The Ned Kelly Films

The Ned Kelly Films
A Cultural History of Kelly History

Stephen Gaunson

intellect Bristol, UK / Chicago, USA

First published in the UK in 2013 by
Intellect, The Mill, Parnall Road, Fishponds, Bristol, BS16 3JG, UK

First published in the USA in 2013 by
Intellect, The University of Chicago Press, 1427 E. 60th Street,
Chicago, IL 60637, USA

A catalogue record for this book is available from the British Library.

Cover designer: Holly Rose
Copy-editor: MPS Technologies
Index: Lyn Greenwood
Production manager: Jelena Stanovnik
Typesetting: Planman Technologies

ISBN 978-1-84150-636-4

Printed and bound by Hobbs, UK

For Lauren, Alice and Ivy

Table of Contents

List of Figures

Foreword

In the course of my academic career, a reprint of a 1910 poster of *The Story of the Kelly Gang* (Johnson & Gibson) has badged my office, announcing my identity as film historian. Composed of various stills of key scenes, the most prominent image is of a well-armoured Kelly, aiming both his guns directly at the viewer. While the long shot rather dilutes any menace, the pose nevertheless links this still to that customary staple of history cinema classes, the *Great Train Robbery* (1903), and so to the broader history of national and international film as Stephen Gaunson points out.

I have been preoccupied by this poster whilst reading the cultural history of Kelly and his gang, across the adaptations and incarnations traced in Gaunson's engaging research. The poster seems to promote a pretty ordinary action film. Stagy and distant in the familiar mode of much early cinema, its awkwardness is the rather mundane under-achieving badness of nostalgic Australiana, rather than fetishised, cultish 'bad' of the prized annals of trash.

At least in part as a consequence of the ordinariness of this group of films (though many would single out Mick Jagger's Kelly performance as an extraordinary moment), there has been little of the invested and informed discussion that is routinely revealed in studies of online fandom, and that might have been expected of films about such a central Australian folk hero: arguments about 'definitive' adaptions, or canonical selections within this wider cultural lore of remakes and reworkings. Gaunson's work resources such discussion as there is more than a hint of 'companion' in his approach, for it surveys broader cultural and academic debates around Kelly.

Australian cinema has produced popular or populist hits infrequently, and means that only rarely does a film version achieve the status of a benchmarking representation of national myths. Instead the field is left open to other cultural forms … in this case novels and bush ballads. Within the circuits of ongoing Kelly-lore cultural production ghoulish preoccupations with bodily remains appear to be of greater current interest.

The status of these films as part of the historiography of Kelly preoccupies Gaunson in this study, one that animates and illuminates an overlooked area of cultural history. Whilst so much of the scholarship on Australia's film history treats earlier cycles of production as quite separate from the revival and post-revival films, Gaunson traces a tangled weave of 'Cinema-Ned' and 'history-Kelly' intertexts, shifting significations and historical repositionings, from the pioneering beginnings of cinema until 2003. He creates a complex diachronic portrait of Kelly, where 'Cinema-Ned' as 'social bandit' moves in and out of focus.

The research brings together a baggy group of films, 'shar[ing] the bushranger's own calamity of flaws, faults and failures' and overshadowed, in Gaunson's view, by something in the enduring and ever-renewing myth of Kelly that defies adequate representation. Yet *The Ned Kelly Films: A Cultural History* is equally an industrial, ideological and social history of Australian cinema itself, its specific ecologies, improvising pioneers, eccentric international collaborations, odd byways, prevailing themes, discontinuities and experimentations on the margins of social and cinematic respectability. It is a most welcome contribution.

Dr Jane Landman
Victoria University
Melbourne, July 2012

Acknowledgements

I owe a huge debt of gratitude to Research and Innovation and the School of Media and Communication at RMIT University for the Early Career Fellowship, which allowed this book's completion.

Other grants and institutions that have provided great assistance include the AGL Shaw Fellowship at the State Library of Victoria, AFI Research Collection, Mediatheque (Melbourne) and National Film & Sound Archive (Canberra).

Those who have provided valuable guidance, assistance, corrections and encouragement throughout my Ph.D. candidature and now the writing of this book include Adrian Danks, Ina Bertrand, Lisa French, Murray Pomerance, Tania Lewis, Stephanie Donald, Shane Carmody, Dianne Reilly, Peter Kemp, Jeff Lewis, Lucy Morieson, Jo Tacchi, Terry Johal, Ashley Perry, Alex Gionfriddo, Julie Stafford, Deb Verhoeven, anonymous readers, Jelena Stanovnik, Lyn Greenwood, Melanie Marshall and Intellect Books.

The Kelly Films

The Perth Fragment (1906)
The Story of the Kelly Gang (Charles Tait 1906)
The Story of the Kelly Gang (William Gibson and Millard Johnson 1910)
The Kelly Gang (Harry Southwell 1919)
When the Kellys Were Out (Harry Southwell 1923)
When the Kellys Rode (Harry Southwell 1934)
The Glenrowan Affair (Rupert Kathner 1951)
Ned Kelly: Australian Paintings by Sidney Nolan (Tim Burstall 1960)
Ned Kelly (William Sterling 1960)
The Stringybark Massacre (Garry Shead 1967)
Ned Kelly (Tony Richardson 1970)
The Trial of Ned Kelly (John Gauci 1977)
The Last Outlaw (Kevin James Dobson and George Miller 1980)
Reckless Kelly (Yahoo Serious 1993)
Ned Kelly (Gregor Jordan 2003)
Ned (Abe Forsythe 2003)

Backstory

On 16 April 1878, Constable Alexander Fitzpatrick came to charge Dan Kelly with cattle duffing – a crime often attached to the Kelly clan from generations past. Some time later, he departed nursing a severely wounded wrist and accusing Dan's eldest brother, Ned, of attempted murder. The Kellys vehemently denied the allegation, as did Ned, who claimed to not have been in the vicinity: 'I was 400 miles from Greta'. Hours later a police party stormed the homestead, only to discover the brothers had already fled. For compensation, they arrested those in attendance during the incident: Mrs Kelly, Will Skillion (the family's brother in-law) and neighbour 'Brickey' Williamson. All were charged with conspiracy to murder. The presiding Justice Redmond Barry sentenced Skillion and Williamson to six years each. Mrs Kelly was sentenced to three years. Any thought of the brothers' peaceful surrender was best forgotten when Justice Barry publicly affirmed his contempt: 'had Ned been present I would have sentenced him to twenty-one years' (Corfield 2003: 42). The Victorian Government offered £100 for the apprehension of the Kelly brothers.

Some months later, reports were emerging of the brothers fossicking for gold in Mansfield's Wombat Ranges. A four-man police party did not fool the Kellys who along with friends – Steve Hart and Joe Byrne – shot dead and looted Constable McIntyre, Constable Scanlon and Sergeant Kennedy. Only Constable Lonigan survived to tell his tale. Once news spread of the police killings, the bounty rose to £500 and the press portrayed Ned Kelly as the terror of the Australian bush. The Melbourne *Argus*, as a typical example, reported:

> *The body was face upwards, and Kennedy's cloak thrown over it. It presented a frightful spectacle. He had been shot through the side of the head, the bullet coming out in front, carrying away part of the face. I believe there are several shots through the body. There was a bullet mark on a tree near where the body was lying. He appears to have been shot whilst running away in the direction taken by Constable McIntyre.*
>
> (1 November 1878: 5)

Six weeks later, the now branded 'Kelly Gang' ambushed a station property – known as Younghusband's Station – at Faithfull's Creek near Euroa and 27 miles west of Benalla. During the ambush, 22 hostages were locked in a storeroom as the gang looted the hawker's van of Sandy Gloster. The van also transported them to their Euroa bank heist. Joe Byrne guarded the prisoners as the others rode into town. At the bank, Ned Kelly entered through the front door with his revolver drawn. Dan approached via the rear. Minutes later they fled with a £2260 booty in notes and gold. Upon returning to the station homestead, they entertained their hostages with a horse show and reading of Kelly's letter, addressed to the parliamentarian Donald Cameron MLA. In true social bandit style, Kelly argued Stringybark as a case of self-defence. He wrote:

> *This cannot be called wilful murder, for I was compelled to shoot them in my own defence, or lie down like a cur and die. Certainly their wives and children are to be pitied, but those men came into the bush with the intention of shooting me down like a dog, and yet they know and acknowledge I have been wronged.*
>
> (N. Kelly 1878)

Dismissing the letter as provocative ramblings, the Melbourne *Argus* scorned:

> *The leader of the Gang has written a voluminous letter to a member of the Legislative Assembly, in which he relates his history, and alleges that his mother and other friends, who are at the present in gaol for assaulting a constable, have been wronged by the police. He asks for no mercy for himself, but demands that justice shall be done to his friends, and threatens to do diabolical acts if his request is not complied with. The letter is evidently written for the purpose of exciting public sympathy.*
>
> (27 December 1878: 3)

Two months later, on 10 February 1879, the gang staged their second bank raid, and while many thought it could not be possible, this was even more audacious. It took place at the Bank of New South Wales in Jerilderie. The previous day they had locked the police in their own cells and, wearing their uniforms, masqueraded through the streets.

They rounded up 60 community members in the dining room of the Royal Mail Hotel, and never letting an opportunity pass, Kelly read his hostages passages from his latest missive. His plan was to see it published in the *Jerilderie Gazette*; however, such ideas were thwarted when the newspaper editor Samuel Gill escaped from his grasp. Instead, Kelly left it in the safekeeping of the bank employee Edward Living who later handed it over to the police. Before departing, they raided the bank of more than £2000, and in a gesture bound to gain widespread applause, Kelly burnt a number of mortgage bills in front of his hostages. After Jerilderie, the Victorian Government and New South Wales Government raised the reward amount to £8000, and canvassed wanted posters throughout the counties. The Chief Commissioner of the Victoria Police, Frederick Charles Standish, also employed the services of six Queensland Aboriginal 'black' trackers. The gang disappeared for 17 months only to emerge in the most breathtaking fashion.

Aware that sympathiser Aaron Sherritt was working as an informant for the police, on the night of 26 June 1880, Joe Byrne, accompanied by Dan Kelly, rode to Beechworth and shot him dead. Inside Sherritt's shanty, four policemen hid underneath his bed, and for seven-hours they prayed that Joe would not kill them. By the time they gathered the courage to emerge, the bushrangers had already ridden 40 miles back to join Ned and Steve Hart at Glenrowan.

The killing of the defenceless Sherritt did nothing to help Kelly's public sympathy; a report in the Melbourne *Argus* titled 'Another Kelly Outrage: Cold-Blooded Murder' stated:

> *On Saturday evening the band of outlaws called at the hut of a man named Aaron Sherritt, having with them a German who they compelled to call on Sherritt to come out. The latter, recognising the voice, complied with the request, and on his coming out of the door he was instantly shot dead by Joe Byrne, who put one bullet through his head and another through his body. In the hut were a party of police, but they did not fire a shot at the bushrangers, and acted entirely on the defence. The reason given for this inactivity is that the night was dark, while there was a bright fire burning in the hut, so that while the bushrangers were out of sight the police would have been instantly seen and shot if they had appeared at the door or window.*
>
> (28 June 1880: 5)

At Glenrowan, Ned and Steve forced railway gangers James Reardon and Denis Sullivan to remove some train tracks, with a plan to derail the Special Police Train as it passed through Glenrowan after the news of Sherritt's murder broke. From there, the gang wearing their custom-made armoured suits, moulded from stolen ploughshares, would shoot any surviving passengers of the crash. Earlier in his Cameron letter, Kelly had forewarned:

> *as I have no more paper unless I rob for it. If I get justice I will cry a go. For I need no lead or powder to revenge my cause, and if words be louder, I will oppose your laws with no offence (remember your railroads), and a sweet good bye from Edward Kelly – a forced outlaw.*
>
> (N. Kelly 1878)

As the 30 Glenrowan hostages were bunkered down in Mrs Jones's Inn, news reached Melbourne of Aaron Sherritt's assassination. It was Sunday 27 June. As Kelly had predicted, later that night a Special Police Train departed from Spencer Street Station en route to Beechworth. Aboard were 50 police officers; Aboriginal 'black' trackers; medical assistants; as well as pressmen John McWhirter (reporter, *The Age*); George Allen (reporter, *Daily Telegraph*); Joe Melvin (reporter, The Melbourne *Argus*); and Thomas Carrington (illustrator, *The Australasian Sketcher*). Because of their hefty equipment, photographers were not permitted. Kelly most certainly would have enjoyed the irony of the press being aboard for on many occasions he had publicly declared his disdain towards them. In the Cameron letter, he scornfully claimed: 'Had I robbed, plundered, ravished and murdered everything I met, my character could not be painted blacker than it is at present'. Two months later, when Kelly composed the 'Jerilderie letter', his views had become more contemptuous: 'The police got great credit and praise in the papers for arresting the mother of twelve children, one an infant on her breast' (N. Kelly 1879).

If not for the actions of the escaped hostage, schoolteacher Thomas Curnow, Ned Kelly most probably would have been historicised as a mass murderer. Once Curnow left the Inn, he made a beeline for the train tracks where he stood holding a lantern and red flag to warn the Special Police Train of its frightening hazard. Narrowly escaping their derailment, the police and 'black' trackers surrounded the Inn. The gang inside donned their armoured suits and waited amongst the hostages. The pressmen assembled under the station's shelter. The time was 3am. Since the outbreak had begun, this was the first occasion in which the bushrangers were surrounded. As sporadic gunfire, from both parties, continued throughout the night, the first casualty was Joe Byrne – shot in the groin as he fixed himself a drink at the bar. He dropped to his death shortly thereafter.

As dawn was still breaking, Kelly in his ploughshare suit appeared before a contingent of the police officers. Needling 28 bullets through gaps in the armour, Sergeant Steele fired the golden bullet – striking Kelly's thigh. Now at the mercy of the police, Kelly's reign of outlawry was over. Meanwhile, Steve and Dan in the Inn sat amongst the corpses of John Jones (the 13-year old son of the Inn's proprietor Anne Jones), George Metcalf and Martin Cherry, who were all killed by the police fire. The death of the civilian hostages was yet another strike against the police. Accepting the battle lost, and rather than be taken alive, Steve and Dan conceded to a suicide pact. Unbeknownst to this, the police incinerated the Inn, and thus, cremated the corpses of Steve and Dan.

Ned Kelly's preliminary hearing commenced in Beechworth on 6 August 1880. The previous night, Mr David Gaunson MLA was announced as Kelly's official representative.[1] During the hearing the Crown's key witness, Constable McIntyre, deposed that Ned Kelly had maliciously murdered his colleagues at Stringybark Creek. Fearing a biased jury, the trial was shifted to Melbourne. Located at the Central Criminal Court it began on 28 October. In spite of his earlier decrement of the accused, Justice Redmond Barry presided the trial. True to form, Barry wrapped up the proceedings by 4:30pm the following day (so he could attend his beloved Melbourne Cup carnival). At 5:10pm the jury unanimously acceded to the verdict of guilty. To Barry, Kelly foreboded:

> *But the day will come when we shall all have to go to a bigger court than this. Then we will see who is right and who is wrong. No matter how long a man lives, he is bound to come to judgement somewhere, as well here as anywhere. It will be different the next time they have a Kelly trial, for they are not all killed.*

'Death by hanging', a victorious Redmond Barry gleefully bellowed to the court. Locked down in his cell, the only people allowed any visitation were family members and friends; among whom were (his supposed lover) Catherine Lloyd as well as family members Kate (sister) and Mrs Kelly (mother). Much has been made of Kelly's last meal that consisted of roast lamb, green peas and a bottle of claret. Joseph Ashmead, for one, speaks of its symbolic reference to Jesus: the bible reads 'give strong drink to him who is to perish' (Ashmead 1922: 28).

The alcohol did little to exhaust Kelly, who according to the night guards, sung ballads including his favourite, 'Farewell to My Home in Greta'.

See, yonder ride four troopers
One kiss before we part,
Now haste and join your comrades,
Dan, Joe Byrne and Stevie Hart.

(Seal 2002: 104)

In the morning, the Very Rev. Dean Donoghy administered Kelly his last rites. A prison procession arrived at his cell, and from there they advanced to the gallows. A large gathering convened outside the gates of the gaol. Family members, friends and sympathisers chose the more private setting of the Robert Burns Hotel, located nearby at Smith Street, Collingwood (I. Jones 2002: 322). Those allowed to witness the hanging were mostly press representatives and gaol officials. As the clock struck 10am on 11 November 1880, Ned Kelly was hanged.

Note

1 David Gaunson is a distant relative of mine.

Introduction

A fiction is a story, a sequence of events and variously motivated characters arranged in a usually causal relationship. Such arrangements of characters and events are imaginary. That is, while based on actual or perceived events in the real world, they are conventionally held to be artful untruths about which we temporarily suspend our disbelief, drawn into the story by our identification with, or against, the characters and empathy with the events that constitute the fiction. While such artifices are imaginary, they nevertheless convey deep truths, or lasting values of one kind or another. This is often held to be an important reason for the longevity of folkloric fictions.

– Graham Seal (1989: 184)

[I]nvented tradition is taken to mean a set of practices, normally governed by overtly or tacitly accepted rules and of a ritual or symbolic nature, which seek to inculcate certain values and norms of behaviour by repetition, which automatically implies continuity with the past.

– Eric Hobsbawm (2003: 1)

Enter film: the great temptation. Film, the contemporary medium still capable of both dealing with the past and holding a large audience. How can we not suspect that this is the medium to use to create narrative histories that will touch large numbers of people. Yet is this dream possible? Can one really put history onto film, history that will satisfy those of us who devote our lives to understanding, analysing, and recreating the past in words? Or does the use of film necessitate a change in what we mean by history, and would we be willing to make such a change? The issue comes down to this: is it possible to tell historical stories on film and not lose our professional or intellectual souls?

– Robert Rosenstone (1988: 1175)

Theorists of historiography generally agree that all historical narratives contain an irreducible and inexpungeable element of interpretation. The historian has to interpret his materials in order to construct the moving pattern of images in which the form of the historical process is to be mirrored. And this because the historical record is both too full and too sparse. On the one hand, there are always more facts in the record than the historian can possibly include in his narrative representation of a given segment of the historical process. And so the historian must 'interpret' his data by excluding certain facts from his account as irrelevant to his narrative purpose.

– Hayden White (1978: 51)

Ned Kelly's outbreak (1878–1880) has always been a visual story, for its timing struck at the dawn of profound technological advancement in the printed press. Different from the 1850s 'golden' bushranger epidemic, Kelly emerged alongside the development of newspapers and journals, interleaving their publications with illustrations of scenes from 'current events'. Regardless of photography being the natural precursor to the moving pictures, there were few actual Kelly photographs to speak of, and not until 1908 would technology allow newspapers to print those few photographs in circulation. So instead, Kelly's commodification was ushered through the illustrated newspaper sketches and sketchers' vivid and striking impressions of the bushranger (Willis 1988: 105). This book will investigate Ned Kelly by reading the films as a continuum of Kelly's visual cultural history.

Quixotically donned in his shield of armour, Ned Kelly should never have stood a chance. Punctured by 28 bullets, somehow he survived Glenrowan, and then, his many manifestations within popular history. At no time has he ever not been popular. Lionised as the great hero of Australia's colonial past – the man who dragged the country into the modern world – he not only seemed less to occupy the dawn of a new age, but be cast as the dawn of that new age. Despite such plaudits, however, his paradox is that he neither achieved nor changed anything, politically nor socially. The tragic hero that did little to consolidate his hero status. Not to suggest that he did not have any ambition to implement change, he simply had neither the intellect nor sophistication to orchestrate such ambition. So instead he behaved in the tradition of the classic bushranger that included the usual checklist of bail ups, police killings and his own tragic death. On the gallows at the Melbourne Gaol, he was just one of the 134 hanged felons who also could not cope with the modern world. But unlike any of these felons (even the family butchering Frederick Deeming, suspected of also being the actual Jack the Ripper), Kelly is fetishised as anything but 'just another' in the history of the hanged, or history of Australian bushranging.

Evidence of his cultural fetishisation, or thorn, depending on how they are understood, have been the films, produced at irregular intervals since the beginning of feature filmmaking; the first was made in 1906. As if it were their intention, the films share the bushranger's own calamity of flaws, faults and failures; in many regards they are intriguing parables of his own troubled life.

The illusion of giving Kelly motion, and seemingly the cultural need for this, is woven into the web of popular history, and cinema's place within this web. To demonstrate this, I will discuss how the Kelly films engage with Kelly history and Kelly culture to create a new history (a meta history to echo Hayden White). To appreciate and understand these films, one needs to return to ground zero, as it were, and survey them for how they historicise Ned Kelly as a response to other histories. Never a deviation from the real Kelly, they kaleidoscope the historical artefacts that forever seem fixed to a historical time. And in doing this, history-Kelly transforms into cinema-Ned by seemingly becoming more dead (deader) or maybe just more iconic (or perhaps hagiographic) than ever.[1]

Kelly cinema is a thorny field indeed because of its refusal to attach itself to just one cinema genre. As a point of difference, the American cinema's historicisation of outlaws, including

Jesse James and Billy the Kid, are generally more successful because they are (mostly) uniform western genre films. The Kelly films are certainly bushranger films, and certainly at one point, in the history of the Australian cinema, there was a bushranging cycle, but as this genre was eroded with censorship in 1911, the more recent films appear as nostalgic afterthoughts to a forgotten genre. If these recent films – surveyed in Chapter 2 – can be defined as anything, then they are social bandit films, which as Chapter 3 describes, remains an undefined and hazy field of cinema enquiry, in Australia and globally. How do the films interpret Kelly history to produce a new popular history? How does this new history invent Ned Kelly? What role have the films played in Kelly's newfound emergence as a social bandit? These questions are important for how the films become cultural snapshots of Kelly history. Working in conjunction with the other communication histories – literature, written history, the oral folk tradition – the films are crucial for how Ned Kelly is re-presented and re-viewed. The aim of what follows is not to champion the films as neglected treasures (most certainly they are not), but to understand their role in shaping Kelly's popular and social myth as a global outlaw. The purpose is to survey how the films tap into the written histories as well as Kelly's visual and entertainment cultures to create their own meta-history, meta-narrative, meta-tradition.

The book's subtitle ('A Cultural History of Kelly History') is the best way to define its general premise: how do the films' own attachment and rewriting of earlier and contemporary meditations on Ned Kelly produce their own cultural essays? To what degree can history films be accepted as serious history? Even Abe Forsythe's 2003 lampooning-spoof, *Ned*, which does its darnedest to poke fun at the bushranger's popular commodification, still acknowledges his legacy as a symbol of colonial rebellion. This book aims to consider the films as important Kelly histories – an approach which has been neglected in the past. It will survey how the films speak to Kelly history, and in doing so, how they can and should be subsequently understood as an important branch of Kelly history. Over the following chapters I will convey an urgency to think differently about how history films (Kelly films in this example) impact and influence the broader historicisation(s) of popular history. Film should not be sidetracked or redirected to other destinations, but included in serious conversations about historicity. Films affect how one thinks about and responds to the past.

The very problem of historicising Kelly is the similar problem of historicising a global icon like Elvis Presley: their myths are so monolithic and mercurial, it becomes an almost impossible task to emplot their narratives. How can one seriously narrativise them when so much of their lore is enveloped by a cultural cringe of tacky commodification? Those who have endured a visit to Glenrowan, or Graceland, will understand the point here. There is no avoiding the cultural mockery that one enjoys attaching to figures of such significance; yet, such mockery distracts from the type of deep analysis that can be achieved. A more challenging proposition is to examine how the films unpack their difficult histories. How do films kaleidoscope their popular history? A persistent question that punctuates this book is whether there is a possibility of a 'truthful' Kelly film. For instance, are entertainment films less 'truthful' (in a historical sense) than educational films or written history?

The term 'Kelly cinema' will be used in a fairly broad sense for it also includes the television specials (including the telefilms and miniseries) and some of the shorts. Absent from this analysis are the numerous documentaries. Besides the logistics in tracking them down, I am mostly interested in the problematical task that the directors face in dramatising Kelly history as entertainment 'fiction'. A further study on the documentaries is something that awaits critical scholarship. The revealing documentary (on the making of Richardson's 1970 film) *A Stone in the Bush* (Sanderson, Glasheen and Allen 1970), however, will be discussed in Chapter 2.

Because I am dealing with such a large locus of films, the structure of this book is always going to be difficult; yet, rather than take a more prescriptive approach that demands each film be treated equally, I speak to the films that address the broader topics under consideration. In taking this approach, the book shifts back and forth between the films, favouring some (*The Last Outlaw* (1980); *Ned Kelly* (2003)) over others (*When the Kellys Were Out* (1923)), due entirely to how they unpack and integrate Kelly history into their text. Because a Kelly historian (Ian Jones) created *The Last Outlaw*, it becomes impossible not to foreground it as the most interesting film for the purposes of this book.

This book is organised into six chapters. Regardless of Chapters 1 and 2 mapping the genealogy of the Kelly films, this book is not structured to present a neat annotation where the films can be filed away under particular periods and themes (despite the films being demarcated between the early and later films). Foregrounded here is how all of the films persistently stretch and weave themselves through all sorts of Kelly and cultural histories. This is what makes them difficult texts to unpack and comprehend. Refusing to sit obediently anywhere, they disobediently venture everywhere. And part of their disobedience comes from them not really doing what the film-makers had hoped or wanted.

The cinema plays a huge role in continuing pre-modern myths such as that of Ned Kelly. Yet more than just adding to this locus, the films, in conversation with other media histories, are forever making the outlaw relevant to their period(s) of production. This book discusses the films as cinema history by surveying their own responses and conversations within the canon of Kelly cinema. Splitting the films between two rough categories (the early films 1906–1951; the later films 1960–2003) will map cinema-Ned's transformation from a bush rogue in the early films to a dandy social bandit of the later films. The demarcation of the films into early and later, albeit porous pools, recognises the historical approach of this study. The purpose here is to explore how each cycle of cinema is in dialogue with popular thinking on Kelly at the timing of their productions.

For this reason, the early films (1906–1951), as discussed in Chapter 1, are more historically interesting for they were chronologically closer to Kelly's outbreak and are more consistent with the sentiments voiced by the historical news journalists. Despite the concept of *early* tending to be aligned to that formative period of the cinema (often limited to pre-World War I), this study will throw a larger dragnet over the Kelly films to include those up to Rupert Kathner's *The Glenrowan Affair* (1951), for they all follow a uniform aesthetic style and depict Kelly quite evenly. As Chapter 3 posits, Kelly from the mid-1950s onwards was depicted as a version of the global social bandit. With the films reacting to this social change, cinema-Ned was more humanised and fetishised. The distinction of the later films is how they are interested in fictionalising Kelly's place within popular history. This chapter takes a deeper look at Kelly's contemporary social bandit representation by discussing how the audience is now asked to care and mourn for cinema-Ned unlike ever before. In extension of this, Chapter 2 explores the complicated plurality of Kelly's popular history and monolithic cultural artefacts by mapping through the films from 1960.

The remaining chapters of the book will focus more prominently on how the films rework, rewrite and represent the historic outbreak. How Kelly is represented to conduct his crimes often determines his status as a social bandit. By exploring history-Kelly's animosity towards the Victoria Police – by honing in on the Stringybark Creek police killings – Chapter 4 will delineate the regular and striking differences of representation that have occurred across the films. Investigating Stringybark's aftermath, at some length, I will discuss how history-Kelly justified the gang's police killings in his two letters – Cameron and Jerilderie – and what impact that had on his popular cultural representation. This chapter will also discuss how the Victoria Police's misuse and mismanagement of the Aboriginal 'black' trackers gave Kelly another prop to establish his status as a social bandit. As this chapter will discuss, the representation of the police has significantly changed over the course of the films. And with the later representations tallying closely to Hobsbawm's understanding of social banditry, cinema-Ned becomes an appropriate hero in comparison to the crookedness and incompetence of the police. In reaction to the police, Kelly's crimes are justified as a necessary endeavour to feed his impoverished and oppressed community.

Chapter 5 discusses the representation of Kelly as an Irish noble bandit and his sympathy from globally spread racial outcast communities: the Irish, Chinese and Aboriginal peoples. It examines how cinema-Ned's bank robbing and bail ups become political acts in which his behaviour is in keeping with the tradition of a social bandit. As Kelly cinema has continued to demonstrate, bank robberies for Ned are an enthralling form of colonial stage theatre and appropriate stage to narrate excerpts of his Cameron missive and Jerilderie letter. This chapter further discusses how Ned's gentlemanly treatment of his hostages encourages his public sympathy, far and wide. A focus here is on what role the folk ballads and Irish folk music play in establishing cinema-Ned's Irish identity.

Following from this, the final chapter concentrates on Kelly's Glenrowan siege that led to his capture, trial and Melbourne Gaol hanging. Unlike the early films where Ned dies a broken and sorrowful criminal ('For better the scaffold than the dog's life we've led – what fools we've been' reads the intertitle from Harry Southwell's 1919 *The Kelly Gang*), in the later films, cinema-Ned shows no gesture of redemption for he has done nothing wrong. The tragedy of his death is the corruption and vice of the Victoria Police and British judicial system. The quixotic bushranger who sincerely believed that he could actually implement change has come to the cold realisation that Robin Hood was just a fairytale of wish fulfilment. Here he truly becomes tragic.

Kelly cinema has always marketed itself as a representation of 'fact' – 'truthful fact'. The films present (by re-presenting) a snapshot of the 'real Kelly' through their restaging of the outbreak's key moments – Stringybark, Glenrowan – by weaving the historical artefacts into their narratives – Jerilderie letter, armour and news imagery. It is true that nobody goes to a Kelly film for a history lesson, but as Nanna Verhoeff asserts, the cinema may 'very well be, rather, historiographic. With this I mean that cinematic lessons might be informing us about the (historical) present's relationship to the past, in its variability… films do not merely present a visualization of history, but also of the meaning of this history, and the positioning of an historical present in relation to this meaning' (Verhoeff 2006: 130). How the Kelly films mine their various histories (film history, Kelly history, cultural history), by building their own history, is the central concern of this book.

Note

1 History-Kelly and cinema-Ned will be discussed as different personae of the Ned Kelly legend.

Chapter 1

'Bandits on the margin of the margin': 1906-1951

The early films maintain the popular sentiment that Kelly's sympathisers were a round-up of the social outcast communities: the rural criminal classes, rebellious youths and his own clan. As Anton Blok writes: 'all outlaws and robbers required protection in order to operate and to survive at all. If they lacked protection, they remained lonely wolves to be quickly dispatched, and those who hunted them down were either the landlord's retainers, the police, or the peasants' (Blok 1974: 99). 'Lonely wolves' is a good way to describe cinema-Ned and his gang of armed robbers in the early films, for they receive no sympathy beyond their inner sanctum. This chapter will map through the production history of the early Kelly films (1906–1951). Although it seems more straightforward than, for instance, how the films negotiate and rework Kelly history, this production history is just as muddled. A clash of competing Kelly films, government intervention, inept scripting, poor casting, indecisive direction and insufficient budgets spawned a cycle of bad cinema, without any of the delicious fetishisations that bad cinema often features. By describing the films' cultural and social context, this chapter posits them as symptomatic of their cultural epoch.

However, it was not as if all bushranger films during this time were bad: during the same year that Southwell was producing *The Kelly Gang* (1919), Kenneth Brampton made the very competent *Robbery Under Arms* (Brampton 1920); four years after *The Glenrowan Affair* (1951), Cecil Holmes made the excellent *Captain Thunderbolt* (Holmes 1955). Why then are the Kelly films so uniformly bad? Addressing this question all the way back in 1980, Ina Bertrand had to concede, 'the complexities of the Kelly legend and its relation to issues of Australian identity make it a difficult subject' (Bertrand 1980: 17). It is no coincidence, therefore, that the best bushranger films, such as *Mad Dog Morgan* (Mora 1976) or *Robbery Under Arms* have not been about Ned Kelly.

The Story of the Kelly Gang

In the early films, cinema-Ned is emblematic of the classic Australian bushranger. Grubby, dusty and a rogue, in description of this Ned William D. Routt explained: 'spawned in poverty, defying the respectable, rough, unseemly and somewhat uncut. The principle of their selection has been, then, metaphorical – a resemblance of the unruly spirit, not the flesh' (Routt 2003b). While many critical commentators fetishize *The Story of the Kelly Gang* (Charles Tait 1906) for its historical significance as the world's first feature film, Jill Matthews argues that in 1906 it was 'subjected to considerable criticism for its lack of exact realism and for presenting the well-known story in the pure spirit of two-penny coloured melodrama' (Matthews 2005: 111). The early films' shoddy quality, and failure to stimulate on any intellectual or aesthetic level, however, does produce an appropriately negative impression of history-Kelly, enhanced further by the staging of his felonious exploits. Rather than frame cinema-Ned on the former of right/wrong-good/bad binaries, the early films are morally complex, because he is forever tempted to behave in a manner that even his own community of rogues and cattle duffers consider 'unjust'. These early films are cautionary tales about the perils of bushranging. As the leader of the Kelly Gang, he is a lone wolf fighting a lone battle: 'bandits on the margin of the margin' (Routt 2003a).

It is believed that *The Story of the Kelly Gang* (1906) was the first long-film and feature-length film ever made. Its original length was said to be around 70 minutes, but sadly only 18 minutes of fragmented footage currently exists. It was not, however, the first Kelly moving picture for there was another produced earlier in 1906. All that remains of this 'other' film is one grainy scene, dubbed by Ina Bertrand as 'the Perth Fragment'. It features Aaron Sherritt betraying the gang. Believed to have been registered at the Proprietors of Copyright on 14 December 1906, Routt understands it to have been adapted from one of the stage plays: *The Kelly Gang or the Career of Ned Kelly, the Ironclad Bushranger of Australia* (1898) produced and written by Arnold Denham, or *Hands Up! Or Ned Kelly and His Gang or The Iron-Clad Bushranger* (1903) produced by E. I. Cole (Fotheringham 1987: 32; Routt 2003a).

Denham's play had inspired other vaudeville celebrating the subject of 'lawlessness' and probably he influenced Cole's own Kelly play (Irvin 1981: 82). Routt understands that 'it would not have been out of the question for Cole's company to have been touring with this production in Western Australia in 1906, just as it would not be out of the question for entrepreneur Dan Barry to have been in Western Australia with his "cold-blooded" Kelly revival the year before' (Routt 2003a). 'The Perth Fragment' was most likely titled 'The Kelly Gang' and was not a feature film. Routt summarises the gang from 'the Perth Fragment' to liken them to Denham's play: 'Vile fellows, not like heroes at all' (Routt 2003a). On the same evening as the Taits' Melbourne premiere, a film titled 'The Kelly Gang' premiered at the Hobart Town Hall. This may well have been another copy of the Taits' film, or just perhaps the film including 'the Perth Fragment' (Bertrand and Routt 2007: 36). Dan Barry and Robert Hollyford presented it. Adding further confusion were the Taits, who promoted their film as either 'The Story of the Kelly Gang' or 'The Kelly Gang'. Confirmation of this other film is found in a legal memorandum between legal associates Gavan, Duffy, King and King, who discuss their client – brother of Ned – James 'Jim's' desire to see the banning of the Tait brothers' Kelly film. He had earlier banned 'another' Kelly film produced in Western Australia (Gavan et al. 1906). Jim, paradoxically, had no problem exploiting Ned's name for his own financial gain: the night that his brother hanged, he appeared at the Apollo Hall, Melbourne with his sister Kate; flamboyantly they entered the stage on Ned's favourite white stallion.

The Tait family was certainly involved in the international exhibition of bushranging vaudeville prior to their film. In addition to holding the rights to the Kelly 'Flesh and Blood' Show (Reade 1970: 28), they toured David Burn's *The Bushrangers* around Britain (V. Tait 1971; Burn 1829). As Graham Shirley and Brian Adams note, 1904 saw the Taits make their first substantial move into film exhibition. Their Melbourne Town Hall programmes were generally divided between the entertainment of imported cinema newsreels and gramophone recordings – as performed by the opera soprano extraordinaire Nellie Melba (Shirley and Adams 1983: 16). Then from 29 March 1906, they had a very successful run with the documentary *Living London* (Reade 1970: 26). By the year's end they had filmed *The Story of the Kelly Gang* (Love 1984: 194). Their Kelly film was shot mostly at the estate of Mrs Charles Tait, in the scenic Melbourne suburb of Heidelberg. The nearby train station at Rosanna became the Glenrowan Station; the Victorian Railway's Commissioner provided a train and gangers to rip up the tracks. (A thorough appraisal of this film can be found in Bertrand and Routt's comprehensive monograph *The Picture That Will Live Forever* (Bertrand and Routt 2007).) Because of film deterioration, a complete synopsis is difficult. Filling in some missing content, however, is the programme booklet: sold for 6d (sixpence) at screening performances in 1906. As this film predated intertitles and sound, the programme booklet would have helped audience members follow the on-screen story as well as filling in some necessary backstory. Reducing the narrative to the outbreak's six key moments, the booklet includes: the Fitzpatrick shooting; Stringybark Creek; Younghusband's bail up/ Euroa bank raid; killing of Aaron Sherritt; the Glenrowan siege; and arrest/death of Ned Kelly. These sequences have remained seminal to the cinematic narrativisation of the Kelly outbreak.

Its astonishing box-office records prove its popularity: playing for five weeks to capacity houses at the Athenaeum Hall in Melbourne, it soon moved to the spacious Town Hall. It further enjoyed successful tours across Australia, New Zealand and London. As boasted by the updated editions of the programme booklet: 'The whole series of pictures were taken by Messrs J. and N. Tait, of Melbourne and London, and have been shown by them throughout Australasia and also England with phenomenal success' (Tait and Tait 1906: 22). Gibson later alleged that the film had returned no less than £25 000 (Pike and Cooper 1980: 9). If true, this makes it (by percentage) one of the highest grossing Australian productions ever. Reducing its further profits, nevertheless, was the Victorian Chief Secretary's decision in April 1907 to ban any screening of the film in the Benalla region (Peacock 2006).

Another Story of the Kelly Gang

Circulating in 1910 were two entirely different films, both titled 'The Story of the Kelly Gang': one was a re-release of the Taits' 1906 film; the other was an entirely new production, directed by William Gibson and Millard Johnson who were the same producers responsible for the 1906 edition. Discussing this new 1910 film, Jack Cranston, whose great-grandfather John 'Jack' Cranston travelled with the film, maintains:

> *Contrary to many reports published over the years, following on from the success of the previous 1906 film, in 1910 Messrs, Johnson and Gibson produced a totally new film titled 'The Story of the Kelly Gang'. With a new script, and almost a totally new cast, Johnson and Gibson's production team set about producing a brand new film measuring about 6 000 feet in length.*
> (Cranston 2006: 151)

Comparing the stills that appear on the theatre posters from the 1906 and 1910 films show two entirely different productions. Furthermore, the 1910 poster makes no mention of the Taits: 'A biograph specially taken by Johnson and Gibson'.

One aspect consistent in both the 1906 and 1910 'The Story of the Kelly Gang' is the depiction of the bushrangers in the tradition of the American Wild West bad men. One promotional postcard from the 1910 Gibson film, for instance, features the gang firing their guns directly towards the camera lens (Figure 1.3); a direct homage to Porter's famous coda from *The Great Train Robbery* indeed. Standing in unison and firing towards the camera lens, their iniquitous manner and villainous gestures create an unsettling miasma of the 'Notorious Kelly Gang'.

Early western genre films had such an impact on the early Australian film practice, and drew such a boom trade for exhibitors, that some entrepreneurial types even produced their own 'Wild West' productions. E. I. Cole's Bohemian Dramatic Company, for instance, commissioned Frenchman Maurice Bertel during his 1909 visit to Australia to direct 13 one-reelers. Eric Reade

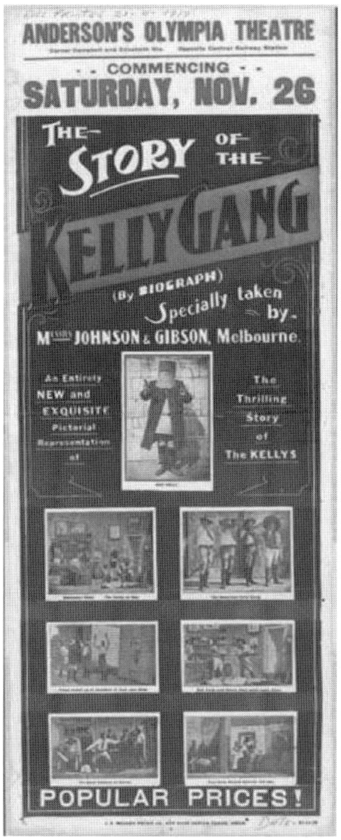

Figure 1.1: (1910). Promotional poster for *The Story of the Kelly Gang*. National Film & Sound Archive: 361321–1014.

Figure 1.2: (1906). Promotional poster for *The Story of the Kelly Gang*. National Film & Sound Archive: 350429–1054.

Figure 1.3: (1910). 'The Notorious Kelly Gang', *The Story of the Kelly Gang*. National Film & Sound Archive: 582857–4.

describes them as 'all completely foreign in title and content to the country in which they were made' (Reade 1979: 10). In 1911, E. I. Cole produced the western genre film *The Five of Hearts, or Buffalo Bill's Love Story* (Cole 1911). With a cast entirely of Australians, the scenes, as explained by the intertitles, included 'the Indian Camp; Rose Tortured, Surrounded by Daggers, Rescued, Buffalo Bill at the Stake; The Indian Chief's Fight with Knives; and, Black Bill's Lair' (Pike and Cooper 1980: 27). Andrew Pike and Ross Cooper understand the Bohemian Dramatic Company to be 'renowned for their noisy and action-packed stage productions of tales from the American West, and Buffalo Bill' (Pike and Cooper 1980: 27). When the Australian state governments began to enforce censorship on bushranging films – from 1911 – many companies, and players, turned more readily to the production of western genre films in Australia and abroad.

The paradox of the censors banning Australian bushranger films was them being no more gratuitous than the American westerns, which were rarely stunted by public bans. The Australian

Commonwealth Censorship Authority assigned the State Censorship Boards – operating in New South Wales, South Australia and Tasmania – the right to censor pictures made in Australia. The aesthetic and moral 'quality' of local films was the censor's central concern. The term 'quality' is important here for the censors were determined to erode what they considered to be 'morally objectionable taste and aesthetic'.[1] The commissioners, during the 1927 Royal Commission on the Moving Picture Industry, strongly endorsed the notion that Australian films must respect the British Empire, for Australians at the time identified themselves as British in subject and character. Ruth Megaw speaking about the imported popular culture to Australia during the 1920s argues: 'Many of the books by American authors which reached Australia also tended to come through English channels, usually in English editions, and thus to reflect the tastes of English publishing companies or the British reading public' (Megaw, 1968: 195). Kelly's anti-English sentiment was symptomatic of what the censor's felt must be eroded from the Australian cinema theatre.

Banning the bushranger

The bushranger ban certainly went further than just the Kelly films, but, the very subject of Ned Kelly only seemed to exacerbate the concern of bushrangers fetishising a life of outlawry – for there was no figure of the bushranging tradition more lionised than Kelly. Appearing much later than the 'golden days' of the bushranger epidemic of the 1850s, he would posthumously become the codified symbol of the classic Australian bushranger – helped of course by his helmet, a symbol to represent all bushrangers. Because of the cinema's profound impact, especially on minor and adolescent filmgoers, there was always a concern as to how Kelly was represented as a felonious binary to the police. Even before the bushranger ban, the Kelly films endured the most scrutiny: 25 years since his death, and still much worry for the rank and file.

The Royal Commission on the Moving Picture Industry (June 1927–February 1928) recommended for the states to relinquish their power to the Commonwealth; a decision that was ultimately rejected with concerns that such an agreement would shut the states out of future conversations concerning the industry's management. The phenomenon of the picture theatre had become a huge revenue earner for the states; and certainly, they did not want any policy that could impede this. Yet, despite the states avoiding the enactment of the legislation (Section 51 of the Commonwealth of Australia Constitution Act), which would give the Commonwealth power to control the censorship of all Australian motion pictures, they needed to enact their own censorship control to appease pressure (from also the police and religious groups). As the 'official' report on the Commission stated:

> *There is considerable controversy upon the effect of the cinema upon the child, and your Commissioners have examined educationalists, psychologists, medical practitioners, police officers, and parents with a view to ascertain the effect and the extent of the power of the film upon juveniles.*
>
> (1928: 18)

The introduction of censorship in Australia, regardless of earlier bans (pertaining to certain films in certain regions), strongly dictated the representation of its subject. Because no concessions would be shown to films that vilified the police, it became necessary for the Kelly Gang to be the story's mongrel villains. As a result of censorship, state regulators would ban any film guilty of the following violations:

1. Blasphemous, indecent or obscene.
2. Likely to be injurious to morality or to encourage or incite crime.
3. Likely to be offensive to the public of any friendly nation.
4. Likely to be offensive to the British Empire.
5. Depicts any matter which is undesirable in the public interest.

(1928: 4)

Of most relevance to the censoring of bushranger films was Clause 4. Addressing the sensibilities of British filmgoers, the Australian government initiated a campaign to erode any representation that depicted Australia as a rogue nation. Yet, mindful that by 1911 the bushranger genre was accounting for more than 30 per cent of Australian productions, and fearing the financial ramifications of a destitute production industry, the censors would review each film, after completion, before deciding on whether to enforce a ban. As Routt grants, the censorship era, until its abolishment in the late 1940s, was a murky business indeed:

> *Even if you did all the authorities asked, you weren't guaranteed a positive decision. Established filmmaking companies were not interested in the risk. So the people who did make bushranger films during this period were often a little like bushrangers themselves. The genre attracted adventurers and people who didn't have much to lose.*
>
> (Routt 2003a)

The 'Welsh Wizard'

One such 'adventurer' was Harry Southwell. In 1919, he shot *The Kelly Gang*; his first of three Kelly films. Not a trilogy of films, the subsequent films were remakes including scenes that had been borrowed from the previous film(s). Born in Wales, Southwell spent the early part of his career in Hollywood before moving to his Australian wife's homeland. Upon arriving, he promoted himself as 'the Welsh Wizard'. Arguing against the importation of Hollywood films, he declared his intention to produce films that are 'authentically Australian in script, theme and location':

> *A link in the chain of national propaganda. Wherever the scenes are supposed to be laid there will the Southwell players and cameramen actually be ... We intend to depict Australian life as it was, and as it is, according to the particular story filmed.*
>
> (Tulloch 1981: 123)

Bearing in mind, that up to this point Southwell's film experience consisted of adapting numerous short stories into scenarios for a series of two-reelers – produced by Broadway Star Features in Hollywood – his ability to form his production company – Southwell Screen Plays – and fund his (debut) feature was nothing short of remarkable (Pike and Cooper 1980: 130). Because of its title, however, *The Kelly Gang* (1919) was often confused with another film – of the same name – also playing in 1920. This seems to be an amalgamation of Gibson's 1910, *The Story of the Kelly Gang*, and Kenneth Brampton's banned *Robbery Under Arms* (1920; Routt 1999a: 247). Because the 1910 version of *The Story of the Kelly Gang* also suffered from censorship bans, the wider public was mostly unfamiliar with either film. Promoted by the advertisement posters, this 'Kelly Gang' amalgamation consists of 'elaborate' action sequences and 'spectacular' gun battles.

To create more confusion, Southwell's film, outside of Australia, played under the title, 'The True Story of the Kelly Gang'. There also were the different versions of this film, running at different lengths. The only known version, held at the National Film and Sound Archive in Canberra, runs for 35 minutes; the 120-minute version seems forever lost. Shooting for Southwell's debut feature began in late 1919 at a studio in Coburg, Melbourne. The Outer Circle Railway line in Kew was transformed into the Glenrowan train tracks; the burning Glenrowan Inn was 'recreated' in a hall behind Pentridge Gaol (Reade 1979: 25–26). In the title role, Southwell cast the 53-year-old stage-actor Godfrey Cass, who certainly had an intimate knowledge of Ned Kelly. The son of the Melbourne Gaol's Governor, J. B. Castieau, in 1880 Godfrey had supposedly met the famous outlaw at the Melbourne Gaol – commonly dubbed the 'Castieau's Hotel' (Reade 1970: 95; Castieau 2004: 278). The meeting was intended to scare the 13-year-old Godfrey from entering a life of crime; and certainly, it made quite an impact on the impressionable child. Godfrey later described the condemned man as 'charming and courteous'. Legend says that Kelly even held Godfrey's hand and whispered, 'Son I hope you grow up to be as fine a man as your father' (Bateman 1980: 170).

In order to appease the censors, Southwell's Kelly needed to ooze villainy. As Mary Bateman concurs, Cass at the time was the ideal stage rogue baddie: 'always played the part of the villain … Cass was often subjected to audience members yelling and throwing items at him' (Bateman 1980: 171). As Routt adds, Cass was big, burly and 'somewhat villainous' (Routt 2003a). On Cass's gesticulations in *The Kelly Gang* (1919), one trade press journalist marvelled at how his 'evilness is strikingly indicated' (Reade 1975: 93). Passing the censors gauntlet in Victoria and New South Wales, on 21 February 1920, *The Kelly Gang* premiered at the Lyric Theatre, Sydney. As trumpeted by a hysterically misleading promotional poster published in *The Theatre Magazine*, it 'smashed all records' (Baker 1 March 1920: 28). Besides the preposterousness of such a claim, this advertisement also promises (or threatens even) to expect 'Five other Productions to be released shortly!' The first was a society melodrama, *The Hordern Mystery* (1920), starring Godfrey Cass (Reade 1975: 100).

Fearing the censors, many of Southwell's contemporaries moved on to other genres and film industries: John Gavin, who began making bushranging films – *Thunderbolt* (Gavin 1910) and *Ben Hall and his Gang* (Gavin 1911) – relocated to California. Under contract at Universal Pictures, he was cast in a number of B western films, such as *The Outlaw's Daughter* (O'Brien 1925). Returning to Australia in 1926, Gavin directed the Kangaroo western *The Key of Fate*, released in Australia as *Trooper O'Brien* (Gavin 1928). The opening intertitle decisively places the sympathy on the side of law and order: 'In appreciation of that noble yet silent body of men – the Police – whose ever present protection makes possible our peaceful daily life'. Sequences from *The Kelly Gang* (1919) and the banned bushranger film, *Robbery Under Arms* (Brampton 1920), were interleaved in a flashback sequence as O'Brien (played by Gordon Collingridge) tells his children about their Uncle Jim, who boldly rid the land of lawless bushrangers (Pike and Cooper 1980: 187).

In the early 1920s, Southwell had intended to just re-release his 1919 version before Tasman Higgins opportunistically persuaded the naive director to shoot an entirely new film, and, of course, hire him as the chief cameraman (Shirley and Adams 1983: 70). *When the Kellys Were Out* (1923) was shot on location at the Burragorang Valley, New South Wales. Higgins's cinematography is the film's real highlight. Reprising his earlier role was Cass,

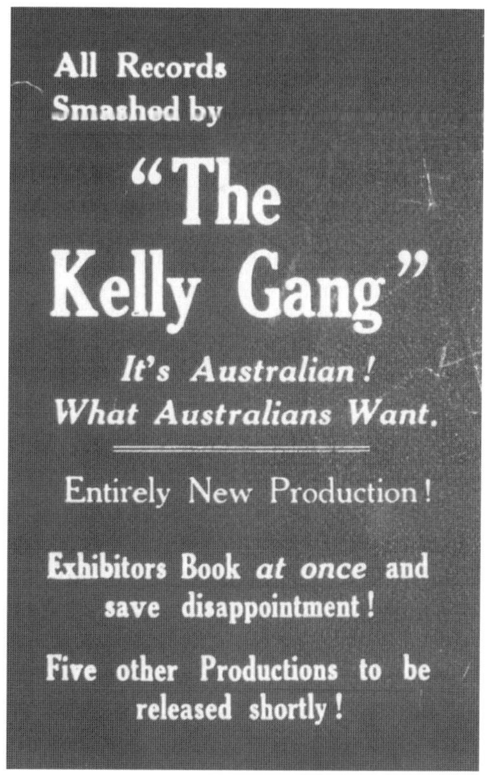

Figure 1.4: (1920). 1 March. Promotional poster for *The Kelly Gang* in *The Theatre Magazine*: 29.

who by 1923 was 56-years old; and despite doing nothing to resemble the 20-something bushranger, his embodiment of the 'career criminal' exemplifies Southwell's stereotyping of the entire North-Eastern Victorian demographic: 'in this version the Kellys and their followers must have been particularly unappealing to middle-class Australian legislators' (Routt 1999a: 247). Unappealing also to the censors, the film was banned in Adelaide and New South Wales. Sydney's Police Inspector, Wilbur Chaseling, even implored the public: 'it is time this bushranger was forgotten' (Reade 1972: 52). On 9 July 1923, it premiered at The Star in Melbourne and within weeks, Victoria had banned it too. As with *The Kelly Gang* (1919), *When the Kellys Were Out* (1923) played under the banner, 'The True Story of the Kelly Gang', when screening outside of Australia. International prints of the film were shortened from eight reels to six (to ensure that it could be slotted into programmes as a B film). As championed by one British trade press review, maybe the six reeler was the winner: '(the) fights are realistic, and the hard riding with which the picture is interspersed is far above the average Western in its genuine horsemanship' (Pike and Cooper 1980: 155). As another example of Australia's poor heritage of film preservation, no copies of the eight-reel version exist.

Southwell next attempted to mesh the Kelly myth within an Asian landscape by outrageously setting the outbreak in the Singapore tropics (Reade 1975: 111). However, unable to convince any Asian funders, Southwell returned to Australia and directed his third Kelly feature, *When the Kellys Rode* (1934). It again celebrates the brave police and vilifies the band of lawless bushrangers. Filmed on location in the Megalong Valley, New South Wales and shot rapidly with a Cinesound crew, it is the first talking Kelly film (Pike and Cooper 1980: 220). Godfrey Cass at 68 was absolutely too old to play Kelly, so instead Southwell cast the handsome and robust Hay Simpson. Unknown and without any major credits to his name, at least Simpson resembled the actual bushranger. Publicity stills from the film reveal a young, striking and athletic beau that was likely to attract a strong female audience. A promotional article from *The Photoplayer* salivated over Simpson's striking features: 'tall, dark and handsome despite the fact that his manly beauty is hidden beneath a heavy facial growth which he is obliged to keep until his part is complete. No artificial whiskers here' (Rosenfeld 10 February 1934: 17). Simpson's new age Kelly was condemned by the censors and subsequently banned in all Australian states. To the embarrassment of the censors, however, a letter in the *Sydney Morning Herald* sardonically exposed their double standards of commonly passing films about international outlaws, such as the British highway robber in *Dick Turpin* (Blystone 1925), while stunting their own film industry (Reade 1972: 166). Antagonising the industry furthermore, the New South Wales Police Commissioner, Frank Augustus Chaffey, quipped that scenes of 'outlawry' are less of a problem in 'overseas productions' (19 May 1934: 2).

As the *Australian Women's Weekly* reported, the New South Wales censors initially approved the synopsis and preproduction notes of *When the Kellys Rode* (1934), only to reject the completed film after the £10 000 feature had been shot and edited (19 May 1934: 2). In a futile attempt to pacify the censors, Southwell published a full-page

Figure 1.5: (1934). 'Close-Up Portrait of Hay Simpson'. National Film & Sound Archive: 574737–4.

advertisement in *The Brisbane Telegraph* (naming Harry as 'Henry') vilifying the outlaws as somewhat demonic:

> *In the field of crime there were no more terrible figures than 'The Kellys' that lawless band who perpetrated a series of robberies and murders with such callous daring that they staggered the world. The picture is authentic in every respect.*
>
> (22 June 1934: 5)

The film in Victoria, initially passed by the censors, was confronted by another problem: following the release of his popular Kelly book, *The Inner History of the Kelly Gang*, J. J. Kenneally had formed the 'Ned Kelly Defence League', to lobby against works that 'discredited the Kelly legacy' (Kenneally 1969: 201). Without too much campaigning, *When the Kellys Rode* (1934) was also banned in Victoria.

By the mid-1940s, censorship laws were significantly relaxed and in response many banned bushranger films were enjoying some public circulation. At the Capital in June 1948, theatre entrepreneurs Oscar Shaft and Victor Hobler finally gave Sydney its long-awaited premiere of *When the Kellys Rode* (1934). Any reference to Harry Southwell (or Henry) was curiously removed from the film, as well as all accompanying advertising. In bold capitals letters, the theatre poster bannered 'BAN LIFTED! THE KELLY GANG LIVES AGAIN…' 'Hilarious first-half entertainment' mocked the *Film Weekly* review (1948: 23).

Figure 1.6: (1948). 'When the Kellys Rode Ban Lifted'. National Film & Sound Archive: 561672–6.

Rupert Kathner

In 1945, Columbia Pictures commissioned the popular and respected Australian director Ken G. Hall to develop a project about a globally recognised 'great Australian' (Pike and Cooper 1980: 265). Initially drawn to the subject of Kelly, his apprehension about the unpredictable (and still active) censors was enough to sway his choice to biopic the pioneering Australian aviator Sir Charles Kingsford Smith in *Smithy* (*The Southern Cross* in Britain; *The Pacific Adventure* in America) (Hall 1946). It would become Hall's most internationally attended film. Hall's decision to choose the dignified Smith over Kelly affirms the bushranger's sketchy social position. At this time, Kelly was commonly codified as a felonious rogue for the metamorphosis of his cultural-social transformation was still some time from realisation.

Not sharing Hall's apprehension about the censors, however, in 1947 Southwell travelled to Benalla, the heart of 'Kelly Country', to begin his fourth Kelly feature – 'A Message to Kelly'. He had previously commissioned Melbourne news journalist Keith Menzies to write the screenplay. In Benalla, while scouting locations, he crossed paths with Rupert Kathner, who was also in the region, scouting locations for his own Kelly film. Wary that another competing Kelly film, shot in the same region, could significantly split his box-office revenue, Southwell lured Kathner over to his film. This at least avoided the duel of two competing Kelly films.

Yet, Kathner demanded to be more than a director-for-hire. By this time he was a known figure of the Australian film circuit having directed four (pitiful) feature films – *Phantom Gold* (1937), *Below the Surface* (1938), *Wings of Destiny* (1940) and *Racing Luck* (1941) – numerous newsreels (including the groundbreaking *Pyjama Girl Murder Case* (1939)) and in 1945 written a provocative book on the Australian film industry, *Let's Make a Film*. In it he echoed Southwell's own sentiments by proposing a sustainable film industry, which appeals to the everyday Australian: 'I've still got to find the real film studio wherein real Aussie motion pictures are made, the place where real pioneering does or can take place' (Kathner 1945: 13). While such sentiments won over some industry applause, paradoxically, he mounted an audacious, and mean-spirited, attack on some of the country's most seminal directors such as dismissing Ken Hall's fabulous *On Our Selection* (Hall 1932) as 'dire': 'No one in their correct senses will say it was a good picture'(Kathner 1945: 36).

Refuting the merit of Kathner's book, Bertrand growls: 'how dare he sideswipe everyone in sight when his own films were so abysmally Bad!' (Bertrand 2007: 11). Ken G. Hall – not Rupert Kathner – is remembered as one of the industry's great pioneers. Forming Benalla Film Productions, Kathner and Southwell sponged, stole and scrounged a budget of around £6000. Shooting commenced in September 1946. In the role of Kelly, they cast the former Australian Rules captain of the Carlton Football Club, Bob Chitty. His athletically menacing stature mirrored Cass's Kelly as an unappealing physical brute. Yet, unlike Cass, who at least had a screen presence, Chitty's only attribute was his tough-guy image. (His thuggish conduct during the 1945 grand final, fittingly dubbed 'The Bloodbath', inspired his nickname 'Captain Blood'. Suspended by the disciplinary tribunal for a total of 14 weeks, over ten seasons, Chitty is still remembered as one of the most physically intimidating players that the code ever embraced.) Football rival and fellow hard-man Jack Dyer quipped about the casting of Chitty: 'it was the first time he ever needed armour' (Coulter 26 March 2006: 15).

With over 1000-feet of footage shot, the production halted after a stalemate erupted between the two directors. Kathner departed and Southwell remained as the sole director. The most likely reason for their split was Southwell's discovery that Kathner still planned to shoot his own Kelly film once the production had wrapped. Because Kathner was responsible for raising most of the film's funds, his departure left the production destitute. Shortly afterwards Southwell abandoned the production. Recovered stills evince it being marred by Southwell's usual substandard productions: one image illustrates Ben Crowe and Bob Chitty in ridiculous beards which are seemingly a concoction of superglue, hair-dye and cotton wool. Suggested further by their codified bushman uniform, this version neither challenges nor amends the myth of Kelly as a vulgar bush rogue.

Figure 1.7: (1947). *A Message to Kelly*: Ben Crowe and Bob Chitty. National Film & Sound Archive: 401361.

Hunt Angels

Since parting company, Kathner was still determined to produce his own Kelly film. Having established a production company – Australian Action Pictures – he wrote his own Kelly script, retained the services of Bob Chitty and cast himself as Aaron Sherritt, under the pseudonym 'Hunt Angels'. Titled *The Glenrowan Affair*, it was shot in the Benalla region. The first film made without fears of censorship it brazenly features a scene of three adolescents gathered around a Kelly wanted poster nailed to a tree. (The tree is situated somewhere in Kelly country.) As demonstrated by their own rebellious act of ripping the poster down, and thus nullifying the police efforts to make Kelly's face recognisable amongst the wider community, this scene's fetishisation is symptomatic of what the censors had feared all along: to represent Kelly as a hero amongst the weak-minded and impressionable. But there was nothing the censors could now do; the film passed without any censorship restrictions.

Consistent with Southwell's Kelly productions, this was cheap and lacklustre for cinema-Ned remained a thuggish bush brute. Even more reprehensible than any of Southwell's films, however, are the quite ludicrous historical errors: an intertitle indicates the year of the outbreak as 1887, despite Kelly hanging in 1880. Surely, Kathner was having a laugh when he marketed his film as the 'true story of Ned Kelly'. The only intriguing feature of this film is Kathner's dare to extend the tried-and-true story by bookending his narrative with one of the tradition's most hysterical myths: Dan Kelly escaped from the Glenrowan Inn blaze and lived to tell his tale.

Although Kelly historians generally dismiss this as fantastical trite, this myth is not new: in 1938, a fellow named James Ryan declared himself as Ned's brother. The book *Horsemen Bold* named a patient of Ipswich Hospital, under the pseudonym Jack Day, as Dan Kelly (Johnson 1995). In 2001, Maureen Tyler claimed her grandfather, known as Charles Divine Tindale, was Dan (Delros 3 July 2005: 25). Jack Allen in his 1935 book, *Burnt to a Cinder Was I*, wrote about befriending Dan Kelly years after the outbreak (Allen and Allen 2002). Kelly expert Barry MacArthur claimed that Ned Kelly escaped Glenrowan and Dan hanged in his place at the Melbourne Gaol (Delros 3 July 2005: 25).

Kathner boasted to having located the aged and weathered brother of Ned. To begin his film, a sketch artist (played by Kathner, who in fact once worked as a courtroom sketcher) takes Dan to various Kelly haunts, including the derelict ramshackle hut that was once Kelly's dwelling. Charles Tingwell's voice-over used for these segments provides a documentary effect in what are the film's only engrossing scenes. If Kathner had instead made a documentary about 'Dan', his film would have been more curious at least. The feature premiered at the Capitol Theatre, Sydney on 17 August 1951. Yet, as opined by the scathing reviews, drama was not Kathner's strength. *The Sunday Herald* sighed:

> *This Australian legend has enough appeal in itself to need less than the minimal requirements of film craft ... the script is dreary, the photography more often out-of-focus than in, the editing is unimaginative and the acting pitiful.*
>
> (9 August 1951: 5)

The 2005 biopic docudrama based on Kathner's career, *Hunt Angels* (Morgan 2006), has given the director some posthumous notoriety in which *The Glenrowan Affair* (1951) is championed as his crowning achievement. This docudrama, however, in the true spirit of Kathner, is also crammed full of baffling misinformation: one instance declares *The Glenrowan Affair* as the only Australian feature released in 1951, despite others including *Wherever She Goes* (Gordon 1951) also premiering that year. Celebrating Kathner's 'Badness' as his most enjoyable pleasure (in an Ed Wood sort of way), clips from his films are interleaved as Kathner experts discuss his shonky methods, bum-luck and financial restrictions. Such treatment of Kathner is fine, but claims that *The Glenrowan Affair* is a neglected gem of Australian 'B' trash are simply wrong. It never enjoyed a 'fabulous' premiere in Benalla; and not only did Kelly descendants not appreciate this film, they lobbied to see it banned in Kelly Country, vis-à-vis the Dan Kelly escape myth being unfounded and deliberately offensive. Reports indicated that every time the withered Dan character appeared on screen, the audience booed and jeered.

Since the very early Kelly films, this body of cinema had been piggybacked by Southwell and Kathner, each opportunistically – and disastrously together for a short time – exploiting the Kelly legacy as a wedge to squeeze themselves into exhibitor theatre programmes. Occasionally, this worked. Yet, as each entrepreneur disappeared from the film scene, Ned Kelly (as a cinema subject) entered a hiatus also. And not until Kelly, as an artefact of popular culture, went though his own metamorphosis would there be a resurgence of interest in his potential as a film star. The following chapter will map through the films produced during this time.

Note

1 For more on this, see *Film Censorship in Australia* (Bertrand 1978).

Chapter 2

The Hagiographic Bandit: 1960-2003

From 1960, Ned Kelly's social bandit iconography began to cinematically sprout. Treating the outbreak as a seminal tale of Australian colonial history, these films embellish the idea that Kelly is a worthy and justifiable hero of contemporary popular history. 'Hagiography' is important here, for it allows the films to excuse his killings, bank raids and attempt to derail a train full of lawmen. Coinciding with Kelly's newfound image, they illuminate hygienic, safe and aesthetically pleasant myths, intended to penetrate an international mainstream box office. This chapter discusses the later films' production history that saw Ned Kelly uniformly represented as a benevolent and noble bandit. Played by young and striking men – in a time of their own prime – he becomes more tragic, for death strikes at an untimely manner. Still on the margin of society, here he enjoys the support of marginalised communities, beyond the North-East region of Victoria's colony. Casting off the shackles of censorship, in this later cycle, the Victoria Police's thuggery and lack of accountability is far more reprehensible than anything cinema-Ned does. Without question, cinema-Ned morphs into the perfect (hagiographic) hero, whose decisions are just.

Tim Burstall

In his five-minute short, *Ned Kelly* (Burstall 1960), its director Tim Burstall performed the folk ballad that plays over a selection of Sidney Nolan's abstract Kelly paintings. A hit with film festival crowds, including New York (1961) and Amsterdam (1962), in 1962 it won second prize in the Open Section category at the AFI Awards. Heralding the first colour Kelly film, the lucid illumination of Nolan's paintings ushered Kelly into a colourised cinemascape that would come to define his modern hagiographic representation. Much has been said about the cultural ubiquity of Sidney Nolan's Kelly paintings, especially regarding the later films, and there is no doubt that Nolan has informed the films, but not to the degree that many claim (Ingram 2006). He, like the films, is part of a larger tapestry that weaves a cultural representation of Ned Kelly as a social bandit – or at least a bandit who must be appreciated in relation to his social and political circumstances.[1] Like the films, Nolan was informed by the historical changes that affected the cultural representation of Ned Kelly; and he readily admits that many of his ideas about Kelly originated from J. J. Kenneally's popular book (Lynn and Nolan 1985: 9).

For his debut feature, Burstall had plans to produce a Kelly film titled 'Man in Iron'. He had already completed the soundtrack and screenplay. In the script's introduction, he identifies a set of character tropes to which this cycle would uniformly adhere:

1. Kelly's youth. He was only 24 when he was finally captured.
2. His contention that he was not an ordinary criminal but rather the victim of police persecution.
3. His reputation for chivalry and generosity.
4. The length of time he eluded the police.
5. The support he enjoyed from the local farmers.
6. The suit of bullet proof armour.
7. His skill as a horseman, marksman and bushranger.

(Burstall 1962: 2)

Burstall's intelligent screenplay, set around the Glenrowan siege, explores the inner conflict of the story's traitors (Aaron Sherritt; Thomas Curnow) in ways that no (completed) film has been able to achieve. Unable to secure either enough funds or a distributor (he was still a decade from his groundbreaking films and esteem as a seminal figure of the Australian film revival), sadly the 'Man in Iron' project was abandoned.

Considering that ABC-television had also, in 1960, produced their own Kelly telefilm, *Ned Kelly* (Gauci 1977a), Burstall's problem was more a case of bad timing than an undeveloped script. This ABC telefilm was a faithful adaptation of Douglas Stewart's popular stage-play *Ned Kelly* (Stewart 1943). While its star, the 36-year-old Australian Ken Goodlet, was some ten years older than when Kelly died, he was a closer resemblance to the younger lean figure, more so than the macho Hay Simpson. The trade press applauded William Sterling's updating of the 'Kelly saga' (Harrison 1960: 261). Screening on the ABC (Australia) and BBC (Britain), Goodlet was later that year cast in the 7-Network television production of the Australian western series *Whiplash* (Noonan 1960): set in the 1860s, the 34 episodes aired in Australia, Britain and America. A decade later, Goodlet's career came full circle when he was cast as Ned's foe, Superintendent Nicholson, in Tony Richardson's *Ned Kelly* (1970).

Woodfall Film Productions

In England Karel Reisz and Albert Finney began to develop a Kelly feature at Woodfall Film Productions, which was a company they had previously formed with director Tony Richardson. Reisz and Finney employed playwright David Storey (author of *This Sporting Life* (1960) – produced into a film in 1963 (Anderson 1963)) to write the first draft. Los Angeles Production Company Columbia verbally agreed to fund the project with the provision that it resembles a 'contemporary western'. Fourteen months later, the belated first draft did not impress Columbia president Mike Frankovitch: 'I've commissioned a Western and you're giving me Macbeth. I'm not making this. Goodbye' (McFarlane 1997: 478). Reisz abandoned the project and instead directed Finney in the MGM remake of *Night Must Fall* (Reisz 1964).

For others, Ned Kelly remained an appealing subject. In 1967, abstract artist and filmmaker, Garry Shead, directed the short *The Stringybark Massacre* (Shead 1967). Produced by a Sydney-based independent company, Ubu Films, it was intended as a teaser for their forthcoming Kelly feature. Shot in grainy black and white, it cast Rob Ingliss (as Ned) and the folk singer Alex Hood. Seminal musician of the Australian folk revival, Gary Shearston, scored as well as being cast in the film. An adaptation of Stewart's play, it was the first film to incorporate excerpts from the Jerilderie letter, as a means to excuse Kelly's murders. Filmed in Ingleside, it premiered in a programme on 17 March 1968 at the Union Theatre in Sydney, with other Ubu shorts *Mad Mesh* (Perry 1968), whose director David Perry was cast in Shead's film as a police officer. Also on the programme was Aggy Read's hysterically outrageous *Boobs a Lot* (Read 1968; Mudie 1997: 105).

The Stringybark Massacre was enthusiastically received at a selection of film festivals, however, the obstacle that ultimately stopped the development of Shead's feature was the announcement that Tony Richardson was to begin shooting his own Kelly film; cockney Englishman Michael Caine was cast in the lead role. Shortly after completing his war film, *The Charge of the Light Brigade* (Richardson 1968), Richardson felt that the timing was right to reconceptualise Reisz's abandoned Kelly project. Some years since his phenomenal success of *Tom Jones* (Richardson 1963), Richardson had a run of box-office flops: *Laughter in the Dark* (Richardson 1969b) and *Hamlet* (Richardson 1969a). He next suffered the embarrassment of producers Albert R. Broccoli and Harry Saltzman cancelling his project 'Nijinsky' just midway into the shoot. Stale, frustrated, and in need of a change, the Australian bush, surely, seemed like the perfect expedition. But first he needed a screenplay.

Believing that David Storey's script lacked perspective and a historical context, Richardson commissioned Kelly expert Ian Jones to work on a brand-new screenplay. In 1967, at the Kelly symposium in the Victorian town of Wangaratta (10 kilometres from Glenrowan) Jones had presented his paper titled, 'A New View of Ned Kelly' (I. Jones 1968). Claiming that Kelly's outbreak was intended to establish a republic of North-Eastern Victoria, and that the bushranger was supported by a wide body of public sympathy, Jones's charming and charismatic image of Kelly certainly mirrored the newfound bandit heroes of the cinema through international films such as, *Llanto por un bandido / Weeping for a Bandit* (Saura 1964), *Bonnie and Clyde* (Penn 1967) and *Butch Cassidy and the Sundance Kid* (Hill 1969). Of further appeal to Richardson was Jones's background in screen production. At Crawford Productions, Jones was head-writer and director of many Australian television crime dramas, including among others *Homicide* (Eggleston 1964–1975) and *Division 4* (Bayonas 1969–1976).

Only given ten days leave from Crawford Productions, it was enough time for Jones to outline a 'rough draft'. But once United Artists boosted the budget to \$2.5 million (Aus) Richardson wanted nothing more to do with Jones (Zwar 13 January 2002). Working with at least a dozen other writers, just ten days before principal photography began, Richardson peculiarly asked Australian playwright Alex Buzo if he could completely rewrite the script so that Kelly is depicted as a wild 'psycho', hell-bent on ridding the colony of Victoria police officers (Buzo 23–24 July 1988: 96). Buzo was apprehensive, and such ideas developed no further than drinking a bottle of expensive champagne on Richardson's yacht. The script, since Jones, had only marginally developed; Richardson and he are the film's only credited writers.

Mick Jagger

Richardson's casting carousel began by replacing Michael Caine with his joint partner of Woodfall, Albert Finney. The part was then given to the self-professed Kelly buff Ian McKellen. (Richardson seemed determined to cast an Englishman.) McKellen at the time was a relatively unknown cinema actor; his films *Alfred the Great* (Donner 1969) and *Touch of Love* (Hussein 1969) were still awaiting release. He was more recognised as a television star for his ongoing role in the series *David Copperfield* (Mann 1969). Before long, the carousel turned to the androgynous (and English) Rolling Stones front man Mick Jagger. Notwithstanding his 'pop' stardom, he was not a proven film star for Jagger had just finished shooting – and was still awaiting the release of – Donald Cammell and Nicolas Roeg's avant-garde gangster film *Performance* (Cammell and Roeg 1970).

The news of Jagger's casting in Australia provoked Actor's Equity to petition against this decision, by reasoning of an Australian having a claim to the role (Zwar 13 January 2002: 36). Ignoring such vitriol, the rock star welcomed the challenge of playing the Australian bushranger: 'I am pleased with the part', he declared. 'It's what I need to sharpen my wits and toughen me up' (Wyman 2002: 346). Yet, if Jagger was hoping for an image makeover, then he certainly did not find it in the Australian bush. Criticism even came from his own camp. Folk singer Waylon Jennings – performer of the ballads on the film's soundtrack – was quoted in the pulp London music journal *Melody Maker* as mocking the pop star's performance:

> *Sheeit! It had the worst goddamn fight scenes I've ever seen in my life. Anybody could whup his ass if that's the way he fights. Looked like they could've given him some lessons at least on how to hold his fists up. He looked like a girl, y'know.*
>
> (Wyman 2002: 362)

This criticism was echoed by film scholars Adrian Danks ('even in the lead role of the charismatic Ned Kelly, (he) fails to exude a galvanising personality' (Danks 2001)) and Jan Dawson ('his flat delivery and diminutive stature undercut the Ned Kelly legend without even evoking the Mick Jagger legend in its place' (Dawson 1970: 159)). Both agree with the view that had Richardson cast an actor more capable of the role, or not an Englishman, his film would have been more credible. Surely.

Because the previous Kelly films had traditionally cast rugged Australian men in the role, the news of Jagger playing Kelly would have been hard to fathom. His similar age and closer physical resemblance to the historical figure seemed beside the point: he was puny, pasty, English and publicly flirtatious with his own swaying sexuality. At one 1968 Rolling Stones concert, he greeted the Boston crowd with the teasing introduction: 'you got a lot of nice things in Boston. One of them is us. Welcome to the homosexuals in the audience' (Wyman 2002: 346). Meanwhile, just one year earlier in the song, 'Sitting on a Fence', he sang words that Adam Block argues are caught between 'homosexuality and misogyny': 'there is one thing I could never understand / some of the sick things that a girl does to a man / see I'm just sitting on a fence' (Block 2007: 188). To rouse the already hostile Australian public, and just days before principal photography began, Jagger in the press conference audaciously questioned the bushranger's sexual orientation: 'I think we're all latently homosexuals' (Frizell 10 July 1969: 6). During this same conference, Richardson did little to instil great confidence in his star's ability: 'Jagger will either be brilliant or horrible', he shrugged (Rawlins 2 August 1969: 9). Peculiar behaviour from Jagger and Richardson indeed, their jocular manner was all the more unsettling considering that Marianne Faithful, cast to play Ned's sister, lay in a coma just a few blocks away. She had gulped a lethal cocktail of prescription drugs in reaction to Jagger ending their volatile relationship. Four days later, she awoke to hear of her dumping from the production. This news she took far better.

In this film, cinema-Ned is a downtrodden Irish Catholic who defends himself against crooked British police officers. Beginning at 'The End', inside the Melbourne Gaol, shot in grainy black and white, the cold execution of Ned is broken by illuminating colour footage of a younger Ned, returning to his family after a stint in the Pentridge Gaol. Kelly ballads, sung by American singers Kris Kristofferson and Jennings punctuate the soundtrack. The most intriguing aspect of the film, however, is Kelly's Irish Catholic nationalism. For the first time on film, Ned speaks with an Irish brogue – albeit Jagger's attempt is hardly convincing. Shot regularly from low angles, to amplify his authority and spokesman's role, the audience's sympathy is on the side of Ned. To pardon his murder of three police officers, and daring bank raids, the outbreak becomes a political revolution that attempts to replace the colonial apparatus with a republic of north-eastern Victoria.

The film's world premiere was held at the London Pavilion on 24 June 1970. Jagger's parents, as well as Stones' members Mick Taylor and Bill Wyman attended. Jagger and Richardson were nowhere in sight; nor did they attend the Australian premiere the following week at the Glenrowan Memorial Hall. Jagger petulantly dismissed the completed work as 'a load of shit':

> *I only made it because I had nothing else to do. I knew Tony Richardson was a reasonable director and I thought he'd make a reasonable film. The thing is, you never know until you do it whether a film will turn out to be a load of shit and if it does all you can say is, 'well, that was a load of shit', and try to make sure you don't do anything like it again.*
>
> (Bonanno 1990: 100)

While his attempts to internationalise Kelly had merit, Richardson had completely misread why the bushranger was so pivotal to Australian culture. This, Michael Thornhill opines, is evident in the film itself: 'Richardson has misunderstood totally the Australian character and temperament. It is no use trying to bring a pseudo-Restoration bawdy approach to a 19th century colonial disagreement between the Irish Catholic element and the English Protestant Establishment' (Thornhill 25 August 1970). Albie Thoms in *Ubu News* lampooned the film and said that '*Ned Kelly* is half-cocked entertainment and half-arsed history' (Thoms 1978: 101). Ubu Productions (to which *Ubu News* was affiliated) had been unable to fund Shead's Kelly feature just two years earlier. *Ubu News* was quite gleeful to report on the film's box-office failure, in spite of premieres in New York and Paris erupting in ovations from the 'young pop crowd' (Pullen 1971: 9).

The best thing to come from Richardson's Kelly shoot was, most certainly, the experimental documentary on the film's making – (ironically) produced by Ubu Films. Suggested by its title – *A Stone in the Bush* (Sanderson, Glasheen and Allen 1970) – the film foregrounds Jagger's celebrity; seven Rolling Stones songs, all pulled from their current LP, *Beggars Banquet* (1968), play over footage of the pop star flirting with female fans and goofing between (and during) takes. The directing was divided between the actor Patrick McCarville (employed also as Jagger's dialogue coach); the actor Martyn Sanderson (cast as Constable Fitzpatrick); and the cameraman Mick Glasheen. Richardson generously donated 1000-feet of colour film to allow them to stretch the documentary to 30 minutes. Costing no more than $800.00 (Aus), it was sold to ATN-7 television in Australia and America for $30 000 (Aus) (Mudie 1997: 246). Also on location was British pop photographer Robert Whitaker, or 'super click' as Jagger affectionately nicknamed him. Personally invited by Jagger, after the pair had become good chums when he was working on *Performance*, Whitaker's Australian photographs were published in the glossy book, aptly titled, *Mick Jagger is Ned Kelly*. The photographs were also canvassed in New York and London exhibitions (Whitaker 1970: 92; Stewart 9 November 1997).

The Last Outlaw

Regardless of Richardson's box-office flop, in 1971 Italian producer Dino De Laurentiis began his own Kelly project (Barber 1 March 2003: 5). Titled 'The Iron Outlaws', he planned to shoot the location work in Australia, and complete the studio footage in his American studio (De Laurentiis Entertainment Group) based in Wilmington, North Carolina. Yet, unable to convince hesitant film backers that the public were ready for another Kelly film, he abandoned the project, and instead produced the Sidney Lumet cop film *Serpico* (Lumet 1973). (This awarded Al Pacino a Golden Globe and Academy Award nomination.)

After some years passed, and bullish because of their earlier success with the 1960 telefilm *Ned Kelly* (Sterling), in 1976 the ABC commissioned television director John Gauci to adapt Roger Simpson's teleplay, *The Trial of Ned Kelly* (Gauci 1977b). Besides a series of flashbacks to the Stringybark Creek killings, the narrative shifts between the courthouse and Melbourne Gaol. Less interested in narrativising the action of the outbreak itself, it exposes the highly questionable judicial processes and behaviour from Kelly's defence lawyers. (Why did Ned's lawyer, David Gaunson, hire the barrister, Henry Bindon, who only had ten months' experience and lacked the necessary skills to recognise the obvious flaws in the prosecution's case?) Compounding Kelly's poor legal representation further was the bias of Justice Redmond Barry, who quickly wrapped the trial, so he could attend his beloved Melbourne Cup carnival. Regardless of John Waters's efficacious performance as Ned, the telefilm was harshly criticised for its use of the narrator (played by Alan Hopgood) morphing from Irish in Simpson's teleplay into an Australian, speaking in a strong ocker brogue, and apparelled in modern-day attire. In the introduction of the published teleplay, Ian Jones growled: 'this involved some alteration of his dialogue and a considerable shift in the significance of the character in relation to Kelly and his cause' (I. Jones 1977: ix).

Encouraged by *The Trial*'s positive ratings, Jones began developing his own Kelly television drama. By the late 1970s, he had already formed an independent production company, Pegasus Productions, with (his future wife) Bronwyn Binns. Despite never meeting during the production, Binns had worked on Richardson's 1970 film as an assistant editor. The first Pegasus production was the 13-part historical miniseries, *Against the Wind* (Dobson 1977). Investigating the English hegemony of Ireland, and consequential impact on the development of the colony of New South Wales, this romantic imagining of Australia's colonial settlement (1798–1812) was warmly received both in Australia and abroad. For his performance as Briton Jonathan Garrett, the newcomer Jon English (who was indeed English) won an Australian Television Logie Award for Best New Talent.

Addressing the same political and social oppressions as *Against the Wind***,** Jones considered his Kelly saga as a political continuum, with the potential of attracting the same viewing numbers and demographic. Still bitter after Richardson had snubbed him from the 1970 feature, Jones was determined to produce a 'truthful' and 'accurate' narrative. Jones initially envisioned his series as 'Kelly Country': set in Victoria's colonial North-East and split into 13-hour-length weekly episodes, each would explore the hardship of a different Irish Catholic family. 'A kind of colonial *Sullivans* (Amenta 1976)', Jones later remarked (I. Jones 13 November 2005; McDonald June 2003: 65). During the early stages of the writing, however, Jones feared that such a concept would be too hard to sustain: 'Kelly Country' was instead renamed, 'The Last Outlaw', and restructured into four 90-minute episodes: each would concentrate entirely on Kelly's journey from a farmhand into his community's martyr. A kind of 'colonial *Sullivans*' was now a kind-of-Jesus-Christ-in-colonial-Australia.

The Last Outlaw (1980) champions Kelly as the people's hero who does no wrong. Given the extensively greater duration, it has the luxury of covering a broader scope of Kelly's life. Beginning with Ned as a clean-faced teenager, it culminates at his Melbourne Gaol execution. The sympathisers are left stunned and shocked that a 'victim', persecuted and hounded by the police, would not be protected, and thus exonerated, by the judicial system. Interspersed are a number of romantic and domestic scenes to portray him as kind-hearted and innocent. The miniseries further develops Kelly's supposed relationship with his cousin Catherine Lloyd. Shot on the outskirts of Melbourne at Seymour, the constructed small-town allowed for a historical panorama of nineteenth-century North-Eastern Victoria. Erecting a total of 46 buildings, this exterior is the production's most impressive feature (Corfield 2003: 159).

As with Richardson, *The Last Outlaw* (1980) also had an eventful time casting its lead. Mel Gibson was the initial choice: handsome, young and masculine (and Australian), he seemed perfect. But wary of his fame overshadowing the project's seriousness, and feeling that the casting of Jagger had detracted from the gravity of the material (and further encouraged by his casting of the then unknown Jon English in *Against the Wind*), Jones cast up-and-comer John Jarratt, whose supporting roles, up to that point, had included *Picnic at Hanging Rock* (Weir 1975), *The Odd Angry Shot* (Jeffrey 1979) and the bushranger film, *The Chant of Jimmie Blacksmith* (Schepisi 1978). The casting of Jarratt also ensured that the spotlight of media attention would remain directly on Jones. In his report on the film's production, written exclusively for *Cinema Papers*, Jones trumpeted his production as accurate, factual and 'the result of 39 years of (his) research' (I. Jones 1980: 354). A 'historical document in its own right', Les Carlyon heralded on the first page of his publicity booklet, released to coincide with the airing (Carlyon 1980: 1). Also included in this booklet were chapters by Jones as well as Kelly historian John McQuilton, who supposedly worked on the series as a historical advisor, despite nobody seemingly able to explain in what capacity. Sold to ATN-7 for $1 million (Aus), its ratings were nothing close to *Against the Wind* (Murphy 1980: 4). However, boosted by the publicity of Jones's best-selling Kelly biographies, it has come to enjoy the reputation as not just the 'best' Kelly production but the 'most accurate'.

Reckless Ned

Perhaps Jones's problem, unlike the comedy films, was his obsession with the 'factual story'. Informed by the children's books, *Ned, A Leg End* (Ferrier 1984), plays, *Ned Kelly: The Electric Show* (Livermore and Flynn 1978), and music, *Ned Kelly's Jazz Suite* (1977), the comedy films are late comers to this branch of the tradition. Yahoo Serious's previous comedy-spoof – *Young Einstein* (Yahoo Serious 1988) – had grossed over $100 million (Aus) and the film's soundtrack (produced by Serious) had gone double-platinum. His next subject of Ned Kelly, however, was somewhat of a greater challenge: Kelly's criminal exploits made his 'heroism' paradoxical, and a harder sell for a PG audience. Kelly also did not enjoy the same global ubiquity as the German-born theoretical physicist. Nevertheless, because of Serious's catapulting stardom, he was given carte blanche for his Kelly project. A bonafide international star since *Young Einstein*, he had featured on the cover of international magazines including *Time*. Playing out his celebrity persona through the media, one intriguing instance was his interview on the American news magazine television programme, *60 Minutes*: Serious-the-budding-reporter interviewed Serious-the-film-star. Zany yes, Serious seemed to make it work.

Serious enveloped his narrative around the 'Kelly legend', rather than the 'Kelly story'. References to Robin Hood punctuate the film: 'Reckless Kelly is the Australian Robin Hood' reads the film's promotional tag line. The script features corny one-liners such as 'robbing banks isn't easy like in Robin Hood's day'. In one scene, Ned stops his motorcycle on the Australian-cum-Hollywood-star of Errol Flynn, who in 1938 starred in the classic noble robber film, *The Adventures of Robin Hood* (Curtiz and Keighley 1938). An anti-capitalist-environmentalist-bank-robbing-Republican, Ned lives on Reckless Island with his extensive multicultural family. To prove that his bank robbing is for egalitarian, and non-violent reasons, he holds up auto-teller-machines and demands that bank-tellers deposit the money into the accounts of the poor. ('I only shoot guns from the hands of those who'd prefer to see me dead'.) In the second half, the bank announces its plan to sell Reckless Island on to a Japanese company (who have plans for the development of a family tourist park). Ned travels to Hollywood to raise the funds to reclaim his land. There, paradoxically, he becomes a Hollywood movie star of trashy violent 'B' exploitation pictures.

Because of Serious's previous box-office smash, and the huge promotional campaign funded by Warner Brothers, *Reckless Kelly* (1993) was the most attended film during its opening weekend in Australia. While the reviews were mostly negative – many compared it to his earlier film as a means to demonstrate where it failed – the minority of support praised its lampooning critique on a contemporary capitalist Australia. Film scholar Adrian Martin enthusiastically, and somewhat cheekily, trumpeted it as a 'must for all students of Australian culture' (Martin 4 January 1994: 52). Serious, in an interview with critic Andrew Urban, spoke about the film representing Kelly as an Australian cultural hero: a 'laconic larrikin with a disgust for authority'(Urban 1993: 31). Its international release was a box-office disaster, stunting Serious's movie career. At the time of writing this book, *Reckless Kelly* (1993) is unavailable on DVD.

Gregor Jordan

The dawn of the new millennium cropped a field of Kelly projects that were all vying for production. Gregor Jordan after his Hollywood war film, *Buffalo Soldiers* (Jordan 2001), announced his plans to adapt Robert Drewe's bestseller *Our Sunshine* (Drewe 1991); the Irish director Neil Jordan (no relation to Gregor) optioned Peter Carey's *The True History of the Kelly Gang* (Carey 2000); the Sydney television director Michael Jenkins announced his intentions to direct the Kelly feature, 'Fanatic Hearts', with the Australian-Greek actor Alex Dimetriadis as Ned (Zwar 2 April 2000: 83). Jenkins' 13-million-dollar budget, however, was dwarfed by Gregor Jordan's 25-million-dollar project, backed by the British production company Working Title (Sutherland 4 May 2002: 12). Globetrotting Australian heartthrob Heath Ledger, hot from his Hollywood roles – *A Knight's Tale* (Helgeland 2001) and *Monster's Ball* (Forster 2001) – was also attached as the film's lead (Zachariah 2 December 2001: 28). Neil Jordan and Michael Jenkins conceded the battle lost and abandoned their projects. Filmed at Ballarat and Clunes in Victoria, the Gregor Jordan A-list cast (besides Ledger) included Australians Naomi Watts and Geoffrey Rush and Briton Orlando Bloom.

Consistent with the previous few Kelly films, Jordan puts the audience's sympathy firmly on the side of Kelly: the procrustean English class system gives his outlawry good vindication. A supposed adaptation of *Our Sunshine*, besides recycling the characters and the story's skeleton plot, Drewe's baroque miasma is deodorized to the point of being unrecognisable. Perhaps Drewe's broken and relatively random structure, woven together by some remarkably poetic prose, was unfilmable – at least in a mainstream classical narrative sense. Or perhaps Jordan felt that the more abstract Kelly films – *Ned Kelly* (Burstall 1960), *Stringybark Massacre* (Shead 1967) and *Reckless Kelly* (Serious 1993) – distracted from the seriousness of the story. Jordan wanted no comparison to the novel – and even declared to have never read it (Eimer 14 September 2003: 15). In his introduction to Michael McDonagh's published screenplay, film-maker and film scholar John Galvin identifies Ian Jones as the seminal influence of this production. This at least goes some way to explain Jordan's hagiography of Kelly:

> *For Jones, the Kelly Gang's exploits – which included robbing banks and ridiculing the cops, were about trying to push the Colony towards a more just society by rebelling against a government out of touch with a large portion of its population. This is the cornerstone of the Kelly folk myth, the one played up in most books, told in most yarns, heard in song and seen in films like* The Last Outlaw. *And it's this myth that informs the John Michael McDonagh screenplay for the Gregor Jordan directed Ned Kelly, too.*
>
> (McDonagh 2003: xi)

As Routt further contends: 'it is the most classical. It tells an uncomplicated story smoothly and with a certain style … an Australian *Adventures of Robin Hood*' (Routt 2003c: 10). His comparison to the 1938 Hood is appropriate, for each is saturated in the classical Hollywood style. Yet, as scholar Brian McFarlane opines, it fails to capture its cinematic magic: 'despite looking well and despite a more than competent cast, the film is no more than routinely entertaining without being memorable' (McFarlane 2006: 30). This could hardly be said for Michael Curtiz and William Keighley's superb swashbuckling adventure. While *Ned Kelly* became one of the most attended Australian films of 2003, its box-office return was severely below expectations. International distribution was nothing short of a disaster. In under a week of its international release, it was pulled from its foreign key markets – Britain and America.

Ned

Benefiting opportunistically from Jordan's 2003 *Ned Kelly* was the comedy-spoof *Ned* (2003), released just some months later. Like *Reckless Kelly* (1993), its star Abe Forsythe wrote and directed; however, unlike the household celebrity of Yahoo Serious, Forsythe was (at best) a recognisable bit-part Australian television actor. Known for his ongoing role as Campbell Todd in the Seven Network serial, *Always Greener* (Lee 2001), *Ned* was his debut feature – as both actor and director. Forsythe had previously directed a number of equally juvenile shorts, parodying popular culture; *Computer Boy* (Forsythe 2000), for instance, spoofed the Hollywood blockbuster, *The Matrix* (Wachowski and Wachowski 1999). Following *Ned*, his other spoofing shorts included celebrating the offensive radio and television rabblerouser Kyle Sandilands in *Shock* (Forsythe 2010); *Being Carl Williams* (Forsythe 2009) mocked the actor Gyton Grantley's newfound celebrity as a result of playing – quite convincingly – the underworld gangland figure in the hit television show *Underbelly* (Tilse 2008). In the press prior to the release of *Ned*, Forsythe described Kelly as a 'cop-killing thug', who is unworthy of his national hero plaudits. Implied also by the film's cheeky tagline – 'hero, lover, dickhead' – it promised a provocative deconstruction of the colonial legend. But, despite all of its banners and banter, *Ned* follows the pattern of the previous hagiographic Kelly films.

It tells the story of a teenage Ned, who leaves the rubber-crop-land of his obsessed rubber-farmer father to pursue his dream as the world's Premier Outlaw Illusionist. Upon reaching Glenrowan he takes a temporary job as the fourth member of the notorious Hughes Gang – consisting of the syphilitic Dan Hughes; drag queen in search of sex change Joe Byrne; and psychotic Steve Hart. Ned's instant fame that has him trumpeted as the 'people's champion' also brings him to the attention of the sadistic (and hamster fetishist) Governor Sinclair. As suggested here, the film is juvenile in every painstaking sense. Reading more like a cautionary warning, David Stratton's review alerted his readers to its exclusion of an 'intelligent audience' (Stratton 23 May 2003).

Despite his persistent efforts, neither Jordan, nor his film, could put any distance between *Ned*: at a convention on the Gold Coast, he introduced the trailer for his feature only to, humiliatingly, watch (from the podium) a scene of Forsythe's film, featuring an image of Heath Ledger's face on a Kelly-wanted poster (Molitorisz 23 May 2003: 4). *Ned Kelly*'s distributor, Ocean Pictures, threatened litigious action (for copyright infringement) and this hysterical scene was censored from the comedy's release. *Ned* (2003) was damned as 'a low-budget straight to video spoof'. But Forsythe had the last laugh when it received extensive press coverage and a Village Australia multiplex distribution. Nevertheless, one feels that without exploiting the advertising campaign of Jordan's 2003 film, which also included a publicity advertisement showing the cast holding a burning poster of Ledger's face, it most certainly would have been straight-to-video (Figure 2.1) (Molitorisz 23 May 2003: 4).

Figure 2.1: Publicity poster (*Ned*, 2003).

Note

1 For more on Nolan's inspiration for his Kelly imagery see *Conversations with Painters* (N. Barber 1964) and the documentary *Ned Kelly: Making of a Myth* (Bennetts 1970).

Chapter 3

New Age Ned: Social Banditry and Romance

The word 'bandit' conjures up such romantic images – colourful thieves, smugglers and highwaymen; daring and heroic figures robbing the rich to feed the poor; champions of the oppressed; outcasts dedicated to taking their rough but honest revenge on an unjust society. Think again! You have in mind the bands of fiction – Robin Hoods, all smiles and bravado. Forget such figures! They exist only in novels and films.

– Stewart Ross (1995: 5)

This chapter will discuss how Ned Kelly from the mid-1950s has been rewritten as a victim of colonisation and an important national hero. Granting that history-Kelly did always enjoy a degree of popular celebration, the positive representations by this period were no longer dismissed as provocative rabble-rousing. Sidney Nolan's baroque paintings – shunned during the 1940s – became widely popular. Earlier books by Kenneally and Brown were reprinted to a more receptive audience: Kenneally in 1955 and Brown in 1956. Then Kelly's armour, which the police had once considered melting, was displayed in a variety of highly publicised public showings: in 1957, it was exhibited at the Police Auditorium; in 1959, the armour was showcased outdoors at the Australiana Festival of Art, Music, Literature and History at the University of Melbourne. Also in January 1965 at the University of Melbourne, children were even invited to 'try on' Dan Kelly's armour (Corfield 2003: 16). A paradoxical contrast was the Melbourne Royal Exhibition Building removing Kelly's armour in the 1890s from public exhibition, on the grounds of its 'subhuman' fetishisation (Oldis 2000: 43; Dunstan 1996: 21).

Film academic Deane Williams understands the 1950s revival of Australia's 'folk culture' as a period of rebranding many Australian myths. In *An Arc of Mirrors*, he posits the centenary anniversary of the Eureka Stockade Rebellion (3 December 1854) as a seminal moment in the country's re-evaluation of its cultural heritage and global homogenisation: 'The international folk revival can also be understood to be a cumulative phenomenon, commencing around the turn of the century with countries such as the United States, Britain and Australia sharing many characteristics' (Williams 2008: 65). As evidence of this, the post-1950s Kelly films can be read as examples of redefining Australian colonial history, via the folk tradition. Sexy, young and lean, cinema-Ned's physical appearance seems to be strongly informed by John Chidley's portrait of Kelly dressed in his silk trunks over his long underwear and special boxing pumps. Revealed here, is an athletic physique: youthful and strikingly handsome (Figure 3.1). Composed four years before the outbreak,

Figure 3.1: John Chidley (1874). 'Edward Kelly in Boxing Trunks'. Private collection.

it certainly questions the accuracy of the early films' depiction of history Kelly as big, burly and Godfrey Cass.

Bandit

From the mid-1950s, cinema-Ned had nothing to redeem because he was innocent of any malicious wrongdoing. Unlike the sort of complex representation in other more recent outlaw films – *The Assassination of Jesse James by the Coward Robert Ford* (Dominik 2007) – that investigate how a cold-blooded killer could come to be regarded as a great historical icon, the post-1950s Kelly films can be easily read as the perfect realisation of what British historian Eric Hobsbawm defines as 'social banditry'. 'Bandit', by definition, is a person 'placed outside the law'; the term 'bandito' or 'Bandoleros' originated from the Catalan term for armed partisans in Catalonia during the period of the fifteenth to the seventeenth century (Hobsbawm 2000: 12). Since the early 1970s, Hobsbawm's social bandit prototype has been a popular blueprint for many historians to frame around Kelly: in 1971,

Colin Bamblett wrote a BA (Honours) thesis on Australia's bushranging tradition of social bandits (Bamblett 1971); in 1977, John McQuilton's Ph.D. thesis discussed the Kelly outbreak as a branch of social banditry. In 1979, McQuilton's thesis was published as *The Kelly Outbreak*, in which Hobsbawm's bandit rubric directly informs his discussion:

> *The Kelly Gang tallies closely with Hobsbawm's description of the social bandit. The gang's members were young, single men from the region's rural districts held together by the prestige of their leader ... his prestige, which was an important contributory factor to the development of regional sympathy for the gang, was based on skills and attitudes important in selector communities but often alien to the North East's urban centres. He was regarded as a natural leader, even by his pursuers.*
>
> (McQuilton 1979: 3).[1]

Hobsbawm's research demonstrates a broader change to the fetishisation of nineteenth-century outlaws. His study began as a chapter in his 1959 book, *Primitive Rebels* (Hobsbawm 1959), which he fleshed out a decade later in *Bandits* (which has since remained in print). *Primitive Rebels* appeared at an appropriate time, for the 1950s was certainly a decade of significant, if censored, social rebellion. Rock 'n' roll, together with the Hollywood loner instituted a codified rebel. By the mid-1950s, the antihero had a direct identification with youth culture because the antihero himself was a young delinquent. He was the leader of the Black Rebel Motorcycle Gang in *The Wild One* (Benedek 1953), or dragracer in *Rebel Without a Cause* (Ray 1953). He was delinquent in attitude and age – always someone closely attached to his transport as a means of destruction and escape. (James Dean was an avid racer of sports cars and often participated in official street races; his 1955 highway death in his Porsche 550 Spyder was chillingly appropriate, especially considering the irony of his participation in a road safety advertisement 13 days earlier. The fact that he received a speeding ticket on the morning of his death is symptomatic of the rebellious antihero: he is someone unwilling to drive at a safe and appropriate speed.) Horses, in bandit films set in the nineteenth-century, continue this tradition of dangerous transport mythologising social outlaws. Always on the move, and always in motion, cinema-Ned cannot be stopped because the police, literally, cannot keep up with him, nor for that matter, even find him. Riding with his gang into unsuspecting towns, he amuses, woos, harasses and pilfers before departing again.

A parallel is the mythology around the touring rock star that plays out the fantasy of the free nomadic outlaw. This is why the counterculture's reinvention of the studio genres was so keen to cast members of its own generation. Before Mick Jagger came to Australia to play Ned Kelly, Nicholas Roeg cast him in his experimental gangster film, *Performance* (Cammell and Roeg 1970). To promote Richardson's feature, the theatrical trailer cheekily declared, 'if Ned Kelly were alive today, he would be Mick Jagger'. And although this is not actually true – Jagger has never been deemed a 'criminal outlaw' – his celebrity during this period does encourage some comparison: the Stones' exile from England, because of tax issues, further allowed the band to be codified as the nomad outlaws. Writing about the rock star myth, cultural scholar Greil Marcus explained:

> *They were men who bridged the gap between the community's sentimentalized idea of itself, and the outside world and the forbidden; artists who could take the community beyond itself because they had the talent and the nerve to transcend it. Often doomed, travelling throughout the South enjoying sins and freedoms the community had surrendered out of necessity or never known at all, they were too ambitious, ornery, or simply different to fit it.*
>
> (Marcus 1997: 130)

Such a passage could be easily applied to the bandit outlaw from a hundred years earlier. They seem to foreshadow the same sort of threat to the status quo. Their significance is one of dissidence. These social outlaws prophesise the message of social rebellion; this is what all social outlaws, whether they be Ned Kelly or Mick Jagger, share. And when they die, or merely stop prophesising, others and other communication forms prophesise on their behalf. Because the social outlaw is made up of symbols, legacies and myths, which take on many guises, the bandit can only truly exist in myth. One knows nothing about who Ned Kelly actually was – only what he represented. His meaning is what survives, and because this myth is so pervasive and effervescent, it cannot be criticised – the politicisation of social rebellion is never criticised – just the symbols, which are being broadcast. Thus, it becomes acceptable to criticise the way in which media avenues depict Kelly historically, because of how his mythology is homogenised to similar storylines, representations, iconographies and histories.

Eric Hobsbawm

The romanticism and hagiography of nineteenth-century outlaws, like Kelly, is part of the social bandit codification, Eric Hobsbawm argues. Taking a Marxist approach to Foucault's taxonomy of governmentality, which imprisons the working class and impoverished, he posits social banditry as a political movement of 'individual or minority rebellion' (Hobsbawm 2000: 19). The bandit's sense of moral justice provokes him (or her in the case of India's Phoolan Devi) to campaign for the common good of their community's brethren. As Hobsbawm enforces:

> *The point about social bandits is that they are peasant outlaws whom the lord and state regard as criminals, but who remain within peasant society, and are considered by their people as heroes, as champions, avengers, fighters for justice, perhaps even leaders of liberation, and in any case as men to be admired, helped and supported.*
>
> (Hobsbawm 2000: 20)

This support does not desist with the outlaw's death. The 'people' rather latch onto other new and operating outlaws; or, gainsay the dead their right to fade into the sunset, and from historical consciousness. New technologies further allow new channels of representing the dead. Balladeers are now film-makers. For instance, compare the concluding paragraph of the ballad 'The Death of Ned Kelly' – 'And so they took Ned Kelly and hanged him in the jail / For he fought singlehanded although in iron mail/And no man singlehanded can hope to break the bars/ It's a thousand like Ned Kelly who'll hoist the flag of stars' (Manifold 1964: 173) – to Jordan's 2003 epilogue intertitle – 'Despite petitions for a pardon that bore a total of 32 000 signatures, Ned Kelly was hanged for the murder of Constable Thomas Lonigan on 11th November, 1880'. The community champions cinema-Ned as a noble bandit. McQuilton agrees that 'the legend survives the bandit's death and passes into folklore. The reality of the social bandit's life becomes unimportant. The Kelly outbreak provides a good example' (McQuilton 1982: 59). The contention to McQuilton here, however, is that bandits pass into folklore before, not after, death (they only actually survive – in a popular history sense – in folklore). Further contention to McQuilton: the social bandit's 'life' is crucial – not 'unimportant' – to how he is fictionalised and folklorised. Take, for example, history-Kelly's so-called dandy fashion.

Dandy Ned

Not entirely a fabrication of the films, historian Keith McMenomy described history-Kelly as a 'good-looking, well-dressed man who had no trouble passing as a well-to-do young squatter' (McMenomy 2001: 65). Hostages from the outbreak also referred to his fashionable style. Mrs Scott was reported to have said:

> *[T]hey told me that Edward Kelly was an ogre, ugly ill-dressed and hideous and I find ... most certainly not the ferocious ruffian I had fancied; but what are you sir, a well dressed, handsome man – a gentleman indeed.*
>
> (Pratt 1911: 175)

Carrington was certainly the illustrator most interested in Kelly's flamboyancy, and indeed, the programme booklet of the 1906 *The Story of the Kelly Gang* included his illuminating description of Kelly at Glenrowan – initially printed in *The Australasian Sketcher* (J. Tait and Tait 1906: 3–22).

> *He was dressed in the 'dandy' bushman style – yellow cord pants, strapped with slate cord bar pattern cloth, riding boots with very thin soles, and very high heels indeed; white Crimean shirt with large black spots; waistcoat of the same material as his trousers; hair jet black and inclined to curl; reddish beard and moustached, and very heavy eyebrows – altogether a very fine figure of a man.*
>
> (17 July 1880: 167)

Further to Carrington, however, reviews of the 1906 film also made reference to Kelly's 'dandy bushman style' (27 December 1906: 5). Carrington's illustrations of Kelly mostly began after Glenrowan, despite some appearing before this time. One of his *Melbourne Punch* sketches parodies Kelly smartly apparelled in a dinner jacket and waistcoat, outrageously performing on stage to an audience of police officers to boot (Figure 3.2). Apart from the *Melbourne Punch* – renowned for its political satire – Carrington's sketches were also printed in the more conservative *Australasian Sketcher*. One picture titled 'Kelly in the Guards Van En Route to Melbourne' (Figure 3.3) has a dandy Ned wearing high-heeled boots, jacket, waistcoat, and hair neatly groomed and slicked back. Looking suited to rub shoulders with Victoria's elite, high-heeled boots was a recognised attribute of his attire. The autobiography of John Castieau – Governor of the Melbourne Gaol – also makes note of Kelly's 'heeled Kangaroo skin riding boots, with spurs' (Castieau 2004: 5).

Figure 3.2: Thomas Carrington (1880) 26 August. 'Moderation'. *The Melbourne Punch*: 85.

Figure 3.3: Thomas Carrington (1880) 14 August. 'Kelly in the Guards Van En Route to Melbourne'. *The Australasian Sketcher*: 200.

A police officer in *The Last Outlaw* (1980) comments, 'is that master Kelly that just passed by … he is cutting it rather flash these days'. The news illustrations, which profoundly inform the films, depict the bushranger as a well-to-do-squatter, who is fashion conscious and conscious of nineteenth-century popular culture. For this reason, dandy-Mick Jagger was cast appropriately. Jagger's Kelly deliciously epitomises the pop star's fashion: during the Euroa sequence (uniformed in Kelly's usual high-heeled boots), his white frilly shirt curiously resembles the very shirt that Jagger wore during the Rolling Stones's famed televised 1969 Hyde Park concert. Throughout this 1970 film, Ned continually changes into a number of different outfits – he seems particular about his appearance. The film begins inside the Melbourne Gaol; brushing his hair at the basin, he tells his reflection: 'this is how they will remember me'. And most certainly, Jagger's Ned is a voguish dandy whose style represents history-Kelly as anything but a wild bush rogue.

Sister Kate

Further to history-Kelly's dandy fashion, tales of his gentlemanly treatment towards women, and devotion to his sister Kate, persuade many that he was an attractive and charming man – a social bandit indeed. Kate, however, helped his cause immensely by going above and beyond the normal expectations of sisterly duty. During the outbreak, it is said that Kate did everything possible to assist her brothers, and even paid for the legal defence that freed the gaoled sympathisers. Kate also began a legal petition to exonerate Kelly of his crimes, which the Melbourne *Argus* reported to include over 40 000 signatures (10 November 1880: 6).

The Kelly films have traditionally represented Kate as the gang's vital bush telegraph, who on horse delivers them food, newspapers and correspondence, as well as leading the police on daring wild goose chases. Initially represented as one-of-the-boys, Kate's brutishness in *The Story of the Kelly Gang* (1906) was so blatant that Ina Bertrand even queried as to whether a man plays Kate in the scene depicting Constable Fitzpatrick being held at bay:

> *It is intriguing, for instance, to speculate that the actor playing Kate Kelly in the surviving scene of the first confrontation between Fitzpatrick and the Kelly family may be a man in drag, having difficulty holding his skirt together while at the same time waving a pistol.*
>
> (Bertrand and Routt 2007: 45)

In the early films, women are stripped of all femininity, and Ned does not come close to courting a female companion, which of course raises a series of titillating questions: Was he gay? Did he possess the necessary social skills to court a female partner? Did he resort to anti-social behaviour to pleasure his loins? – that is, did he rape? Kelly's brother Jim peculiarly aroused curious minds in the 1920s by declaring 'my brother Ned was so devoted to his mother that he had no "girl"' (Kenneally 1969: 202). Ned's celibacy (there is no evidence in the early films to the contrary) means that he remains devoted to his fellow bushranger mates, and female family members. The only females to show him any affection, or attention, are his mother and (stockwoman) sister – the ones that are obliged to show him affection and attention.

This is only true of the early films, however. In the later films, Ned's horde of female admirers evinces the public adoration, far-and-wide. And certainly, history-Kelly during the outbreak was often represented as freewheeling. In the folk ballad, 'My Name is Edward Kelly', he gloats: 'Oh I am young and in my prime, I'm twenty-four years old. I spent some time in vanity among young girls so bold' (Manifold 1964: 64). Such examples are plentiful: the infamous autobiography, supposedly written by Dan Kelly, also fantasises about the female frenzy that surrounded his brother: 'Ned was treated as a hero and a king, he had hardly dismounted when he was surrounded by my sisters and their female friends, and rapturously embraced' (Pratt 1911: 105). Such regard by the by was not echoed in the printed press that reviled Kelly as some sort of whoremonger:

> *[A]lthough he had just received a peace offering from the manager of the bank at Euroa of £2000. Ned prefers knocking it down amongst the harlots, in whose sweet society he is now basking, and where he will remain till cleared out. Ned would be an honoured guest in any of the Stephen street slums.*
>
> (11 January 1879: 8)[2]

Because of cinema-Ned's Don Juan aura, 'harlots' (that themselves share the experience of being social outcasts) are not a necessity in the later films. Coalescing many racial and socio-economic demographics, in Richardson's 1970 film, Ned only requires one corny line to seduce the wife of the Euroa bank manager, Mrs Scott:

NED KELLY: *Kissing a man without a beard is like eating porridge without salt. Do you ever eat porridge without salt, Mrs Scott?*

MRS SCOTT: *Oh never, Mr Kelly.*

At no time in the history of Kelly's cultural tradition has he not been gentlemanly towards women; during the Euroa raid, in *The Story of the Kelly Gang* (1906), he tips his hat to the female hostages as they file into the barn. Pioneering this representation was Kelly's own Jerilderie letter that ordered his enemies to give '10 pounds out of every 100 to the widow and orphan fund … for I am a widow's son, and my orders must be obeyed'. One delicious tale from the outbreak tells of his escort of the Jerilderie police wives to Sunday church as their husbands sat shackled in their own cells. Comically depicted in *Ned Kelly* (1970) and *The Last Outlaw* (1980), this famous tale is used as proof of Kelly's gentlemanly nature. Joseph Ashmead even marvelled at how Kelly 'joined in the devotional service solemnly repeating the prayers and in every way joining with the worshippers' (Ashmead 1922: 19). Also championing this cheeky incident was the 1879 'The Ballad of the Kelly Gang':

They spent the day most pleasantly, had plenty of good cheer
With fried beef steak and onions, tomato sauce and beer
The ladies in attendance indulged in pleasant talk
And just to ease the troopers' minds, they took them for a walk

(Manifold 1964: 73)

Catherine Lloyd

Regardless of Ned's freewheeling however, in every one of the recent films (comedies included), he has a steady girlfriend. In Richardson's *Ned Kelly* (1970) and *The Last Outlaw* (1980), she is his cousin Catherine Lloyd that Jones has continued to assert as history-Kelly's real-life lover:

[O]ther girls had caught Ned's eye … but it was Kate Lloyd who he truly loved – one of the clan, already bonded with him by the blood of the Quinns and the race memory of another landscape still green in straw-dry summers.

(I. Jones 2002: 229–230)

Intermarriage, as the Melbourne *Argus* opined, was an inevitable by-product of the ill-bred:

[B]ut it shows how widely extended are the ramifications of three families which have been continually intermarrying, so that all over the district the four desperadoes now in the ranges

have people connected with them by blood and marriage, and who are willing to give them every aid and assistance.

(11 November 1878: 7)[3]

Kelly's supposed relationship with Miss Lloyd was the talk of much press gossip and innuendo. The front page of *The Australian Pictorial Weekly*, as a case in point, features an intimate portrait of Catherine wiping her handkerchief against her weeping eyes before Ned, who lies barefooted and wounded on a horse-cart (Figure 3.4). Allowing no privacy here is this motley-crew of gathered men – eye-witnesses to the circulating rumours of the couple's relationship. Catherine's evident weeping posits Kelly as a figure worthy of lament and sorrow.

Catherine Lloyd and Kelly's affair, despite being based on idle-gossip, has remained a titillating myth of the tradition. A blubbering Ned in *The Last Outlaw* (1980) stands before her in his gaol cell declaring his love: 'for the first time I know what the future holds, but it is nothing I can share with you … there is nothing I can even give you except this'. Taking

THE AUSTRALIAN PICTORIAL WEEKLY
AN ILLUSTRATED NEWSPAPER.

No. 5. MELBOURNE, SATURDAY, JULY 10, 1880. PRICE 3D. PER YEAR, 12s.

PARTING OF NED KELLY AND HIS COUSIN, MISS LLOYD.
At Benalla Railway Station.

Figure 3.4: (1880) 10 July. 'Parting of Ned Kelly and His Cousin, Miss Lloyd'. *The Australian Pictorial Weekly*: Front Cover.

off his ring, and slipping it onto her wedding finger, it, at least symbolically, proposes that he did marry before his death. Offering a more matter-of-fact staging of Kelly's marriage, however, is Richardson's 1970 *Ned Kelly*. At the Melbourne Gaol, Father O'Hea conducts a secret ceremony inside Ned's gaol cell. (Although Richardson uses the name Caitlyn, there is no doubt that this character is in reference to Catherine Lloyd for he does not attempt to depict her any differently from the historical figure.) In each of these films, Catherine (Caitlyn) Lloyd behaves like Kelly's doting wife: in *The Last Outlaw* (1980) she brings homemade gifts of hand-knitted jumpers; in Richardson's 1970 film she travels with the gang as an 'unofficial' member. Never stepping outside her accepted sexual role, she curiously resembles somebody like Maria Bonita who was the wife of the Brazilian bandit Virgulino Ferrerira da Salvia Lampiào. On Maria, Hobsbawm writes how she was known to have 'embroidered, sewed, cooked, sang, danced and had children in the middle of the bush … she was satisfied to follow her husband … in general she merely looked on' (Hobsbawm 2000: 147).

Julia Cook

Despite Catherine masquerading as the lawful matron, her kinship to cinema-Ned only supports the myth of him being an uncivilised bush bumpkin who could never attract anyone beyond his own clan. To provide a different depiction, however, and amplify Ned's wide appeal, Gregor Jordan's 2003 film involves his (fictional) relationship with the wife of a gentry Englishman, Julia Cook. Regardless of Robert Drewe's *Our Sunshine* being the brain-child of 'Mrs C' (as he dubs her), nothing deflected from the criticism that Jordan and his producers were forced to bear regarding this. (Literature has always been a more welcoming haven for Ned's 'fictional' girlfriend. Novels *The Girl Who Helped Ned Kelly* (Taylor 1929), *Ned Kelly and the City of Bees* (Keneally 1978), *Our Sunshine* (Drewe 1991) and *The True History of the Kelly Gang* (Carey 2000) all include make-believe relationships to portray the bushranger as a healthy red-blooded heterosexual male. And all seem immune to criticism regarding such fictions and relations.)

One reason why history films are not granted the same concessions as literature taps directly into the dual responsibility of the film-maker – expected to be both historically accurate and aesthetically entertaining. The 'historically accurate' component of this duality stunts them from really delving into the myth and legacy of the legend. On this point, the comedies *Reckless Kelly* (1993) and *Ned* (2003) have greater freedom; after all, they are comedies and not 'serious' additions to Kelly history anyway. Because their plots are fantastically inaccurate (as far as the historical story is concerned), to criticise the inclusion of a fictional lover, on top of all their other fictions, would seem somewhat superfluous. This being said, however, the comedies intriguingly illustrate a uniform representation regarding cinema-Ned's girlfriend. Whether it is the American Shakespearean devotee of Robin Banks in *Reckless Kelly* (1993) or Muffy, the debuting prostitute in *Ned* (2003), she has remained a purified beauty. While Muffy may challenge this representation, vis-à-vis working at the local brothel – 'Slut Palace' – her attire of virgin white and (so we are told) celibacy distances her from the other vulgar harlots employed at the whorehouse. Her apparent nervousness, as she is paraded onto the stage, is necessary to affirm her awkwardness at attempting to convincingly play the trollop. Ned's own immaturities to sex, and virgin state, makes Muffy's decision to leave the 'palace' and devote herself to the bandit's cause (and sexual fetishes) seem rather appropriate.

Julia Cook importantly behaves in the uniform manner expected of cinema-Ned's lover. ('Don't make me grieve for you', she begs). Besides her class division, Hobsbawm would consider Julia as the typical 'bandit lover', whose duties are to 'merely look on … urging her husband to not take too many risks' (Hobsbawm 2000: 147). The responsibility of the bandit lover is to lay low and pray that he is given amnesty so he can enjoy Hobsbawm's fifth rule of noble banditry: 'if he survives, he returns to his people as an honourable citizen and member of the community' (Hobsbawm 2000: 47). But more than just worry about their bandits, they also offer a sort of utopian escape, and, if only for a fleeting moment, let them forget about their fate: Julia's beautiful flowing hair, cleanliness and preferred colour of white creates an illusion of utopia that becomes all the more utopian when Ned is outlawed and unable to obtain her beauty.

A delicious incentive of this affair is Ned's sweet retribution on Richard, Julia's husband, who does little to mask his contempt. Before becoming an auxiliary member of the Kelly hunt, he hires Ned as his stable-hand. Ned offering, in front of Julia, to tame his 'wild mare' (euphemisms are aplenty) provokes Richard to shoot the mare dead with the couple bearing witness. Richard's callous act is a trope to draw Julia further towards Ned: both share an equal love of horses – a motif used in a variety of sexually teasing scenes. To initiate their relationship, Julia treating her horse for colic asks Ned to hold its 'thing': 'I'm glad it's not me … you look like you've done this kind of thing before', Ned cheekily responds. 'Only on horses', she flirtatiously replies. Julia's willingness to dirty-her-hands and be one-with-nature, as well as being someone who enjoys a sexually provocative repartee, makes them a perfect match. The horse barn where they consummate their relationship is indeed apt.

The earnestness of Jordan's 2003 film meant that its criticism was more fierce. As an explanation to justify the Julia Cook character, Gregor Jordan said: 'in the interests of making a compelling film, we've taken liberties with certain elements of the story' (Frost 2006: 250). Because of how Julia was able to distort and stretch some notions about Kelly's sexuality makes her inclusion worthwhile. Julia's attraction to Ned allows the film to complicate its Irish/English binary by spreading Ned's appeal beyond just poor Irish selectors and kin of his clan. But different from Mrs Scott in Richardson's film, who just enjoys a bit of rollicking fun with Ned, Julia's relationship is more of an affair (in the traditional sense of the term), which, due to Ledger's then girlfriend, Naomi Watts, cast as Julia, increases the intensity and verisimilitude of their steamy relationship.

With the couple publicly and frequently embracing during publicity junkets of the film's release, plus their often joint interviews, the general filmgoer came with the understanding that the actors were essentially acting out a cinematic version of their own public affair. Not surprisingly, as is generally the case, shortly after the film's promotion wrapped, so did their relationship. However, one should not dismiss their public relationship as otiose, for it answers some peculiar deficiencies in the script, such as why these relative strangers are capable of such an intense affair in such a short space of (screen) time. Stars have always been a difficult (yet necessary) part of the history film (any history film). Yet the real question to ask here is what stars such as Heath Ledger and Naomi Watts are able to do to Kelly history? How does Heath Ledger allow history-Kelly to be conceived as a lovable and likable social bandit? Cinema-Ned's sympathy, benevolence and sexual allure is what defines his social bandit identity and reason for why 'stars' such as Ledger (or Jagger) become so important to his modern-day mythology.

Notes

1 McQuilton's PhD thesis of the same name is held at the University of Melbourne (McQuilton 1977).

2 However, as Castles notes, *The Age* contemptuously dismissed Ned's legion of female fans as simply 'weak minded' (Castles 2005: 207).

3 For more on this see: *What a Life! The Life and Adventures of Australia's Notorious Bushranger* (Farwell 1970).

Chapter 4

Outlawed: Stringybark and the Jerilderie Letter

The 'career' of a bandit almost always begins with some incident, which is not in itself grave, but drives him into outlawry: a police charge for some offence brought against the man rather than for the crime; false testimony; judicial error or intrigue; an unjust sentence to forced residence (confino), or one felt to be unjust.

Rinascita (Hobsbawm 1959: 16)

How do the films represent the key moments of the Kelly outbreak? This question will be asked across the chapters to follow. Ned Kelly said that he was wronged from the start – said that Constable Fitzpatrick's accusation of attempted murder was a lie. How cinema-Ned is established as an outlaw depends on how the outbreak begins in the films. As a social bandit, he is a victim from the start. This chapter will examine the filmic representation of the moments that led to his outbreak – the Fitzpatrick incident and Stringybark Creek police killings – and how this established a clear duel between Kelly and the Victoria Police. Over time, the representation of the police has changed as radically as that of Ned Kelly. As Kelly has become more heroic and more noble, the police have become more crooked and more dishonest. This chapter will examine how the police in the later films force cinema-Ned into the role of a social bandit. In these films, their behaviour directly echoes history-Kelly's own accusations of hounding and injustice as he claimed in his Jerilderie letter.

Victoria Police

Over the history of Kelly cinema, the police have been represented in two ways: the tireless saviours of law and order (the early movies), or the villains (the later movies): 'The greatest thieves and liars the sun ever shone on are the Victorian police', Ned bellows to his Jerilderie hostages in Jordan's 2003 film. John McQuilton would certainly argue that the later movies provide a more historically accurate representation of the police, for he claims how their behaviour allows Kelly to meet Hobsbawm's criteria of social banditry. McQuilton's account of the police posted at the Greta Station resembles more a gang mob than a regulated police force (McQuilton 1988: 48); however, there are many positive stories about the police from the outbreak: Senior Constable Kelly (no relation), for instance, organised a fund so the local storekeeper could provide the Kelly girls 'with any necessaries they might require' (Castles 2005: 118). Yet in the later films, such stories are ignored to reduce the narratives to histrionic melodrama: the bullyboy police are incompetent, poltroon and crooked; they drink, gang-bash suspects and show no courtesy towards womenfolk. The 1970 *Ned Kelly* and *The Last Outlaw* (1980), as evidence of this, restage the 1877 Greta officers' bashing of history-Kelly. On this incident, Kelly in the Cameron missive vilified their actions as procrustean: 'Fitzpatrick, Sergeant Whelan, Constable Day, and King the bootmaker once tried to handcuff me at Benalla, and when they could not, Fitzpatrick tried to choke me. Lonigan caught me by the privates and would have killed me, but was not able' (N. Kelly 1878). This incident, not surprisingly, does not feature in any of the early films. Ina Bertrand claims how police bashings are a relatively recent feature of Kelly cinema (Bertrand 1978: 164). The gang in the early films are the thugs, and felonious thugs to boot. An intertitle – making appearances in both *The Kelly Gang* (1919) and *When the Kellys Were Out* (1923) – righteously explains: 'Prior to the formation of the notorious Kelly Gang the family caused endless trouble to the Police, who suspected the brothers of cattle duffing'.

Cattle duffing (or thieving), however, is not the worse crime to commit. (In the silent John Ford western genre film, *3 Bad Men* (1926), the intertitle ribs: 'Mike Costigan and "Spade" Allen weren't exactly thieves – but they had a habit of finding horses that nobody had lost'.) In his paper on the early bushranger films, 'More Australian than Aristotelian', Routt opines 'it is not the thieving of cattle that is marked as wrong in this story, but the law that condemns the cattle thief' (Routt December 2001). This is certainly how duffing has been interpreted, and even in Harry Southwell's films where cattle duffing is a more 'serious' felony, the gang laugh it off as a symptom of the daily grind. In the wider tradition of Australian bushranging, duffing has remained an acceptable, and not-too-serious, necessity of rural impoverishment. Barring the comedies that do not go there, the only film to excuse cinema-Ned's duffing is Jordan's 2003 *Ned Kelly*. Although the gang do stage what can only be described, in black-and-white terms, as 'cattle duffing', the viewer is given strong evidence to exonerate them of any wrongdoing and 'actual theft'. Their crime is only to retrieve stolen horses – stolen by the Greta police. 'I'm telling ya something now boys', Ned implores his bush pals, 'I'm not gonna let these bloody maggots get a hold over me'. And so, in a rather exciting sequence of chivalrous grandeur, they repossess *their* horses, along with some police cattle as compensation for their trouble.

Fitzpatrick incident

Hobsbawm's first noble robber criterion is to 'begin his career of outlawry not by crime, but as the victim of injustice, or through being persecuted by the authorities for some act which they, but not the custom of his people, consider as criminal' (Hobsbawm 2000: 47). To represent Kelly as a social bandit type, he must be innocent of Fitzpatrick's charge of attempted murder. No matter what period of cinema, the character of Constable Fitzpatrick has remained a symptom of the constabulary's crookedness and dishonesty. Remembered as the outbreak's catalyst – despite history-Kelly pleading innocence of the botched murder attempt – whether he did or did not shoot Kelly in the wrist has never been entirely represented one way or the other. The 1978 children's book *Bold Ned Kelly*, for instance, has him shoot Fitzpatrick – point-blank (Johnson 1977: 12). Faithful to the sentiments voiced in history-Kelly's letters – 'Fitzpatrick shall be the cause of greater slaughter to the rising generation than St. Patrick was to the snakes and toads of Ireland' (N. Kelly 1878) – the Fitzpatrick incident has always painted Kelly in a more sympathetic light.

The Fitzpatrick sequence remains as one of the only surviving scenes left from Tait's fragmented 1906 *Story of the Kelly Gang*; and because of this, considerable time has been devoted to analysing it. One consistency of the Fitzpatrick incident, across all of the films, is the Constable's manhandling of Ned's Sister Kate, and often Mrs Kelly also. In this 1906 film, he shoves and wrestles with both women in behaviour that one would expect from a thuggish brute. 'And in this way a film about the Kelly Gang begins as the story of two decent and brave women whose home is invaded by corrupt representatives of the law', Bertrand and Routt opine in their comprehensive analysis of the sequence (Bertrand and Routt 2007: 68). Ned is only protecting his women folk, and because of this, he is always granted a degree of benevolence, regardless of his criminality later on.

In Jordan's 2003 film, to put some distance between Ned and the Constable, as Fitzpatrick arrives at the Kelly abode Jordan cuts to Ned enjoying a rollicking in the hay with Julia Cook in her horse's barn. Cutting back to a drunken Fitzpatrick making a frivolous pass at Kate Kelly, his attempted murder accusation becomes pathetic retribution for desires not fulfilled: an earlier scene at the tavern has Fitzpatrick making another frivolous pass at Kate, which Ned, this time, is there to intervene. Appearing from nowhere he positions himself between his sister and the Constable. The staging here illustrates a transparent equation for Fitzpatrick: remove the Kelly brothers and Kate is his for the taking. Such thinking encourages the Constable's motivation to arrest Dan for cattle duffing (duffing of the police horses) and accuse Ned of attempted murder.

In Richardson's 1970 film, Fitzpatrick in the commotion of being pulled away from Kate, shoots his own wrist after Dan hollers 'look its Ned'. Laughing off the incident and accepting the Kellys' liquor, the sheepish Constable fibs 'I promise you won't hear a word about it, not a word'. From here, Richardson cuts to a small army of police officers led by Fitzpatrick riding towards the Kelly homestead. In Harry Southwell's *When the Kellys Were Out* (1923), Fitzpatrick becomes more sympathetic: 'I must do my duty Mrs Kelly' the intertitle transcribes. Storming in to break up the mêlée, in a wrestle for Fitzpatrick's pistol, the Constable is shot (by his own hand) in the wrist. Now with possession of the weapon, Ned points Fitzpatrick to the door from which he came. 'Some day - I'll square it' the intertitle ominously forebodes. Similar words are spoken by the departing Fitzpatrick in Jordan's 2003 film: 'I'll be back for ya, ya damned scum!' After the attempted murder accusation is made, Ned furiously bellows:

> *They take the word of a lying drunkard and arrest an innocent woman. Well, I tell you, I will not accept this injustice ... because it's wrong. This treatment is wrong. I'll kill him. I'll scatter his blood and brains like rain, I swear.*

Because Fitzpatrick is always depicted as small (physically to emphasise the point) and paltry, he becomes swallowed by the enormity and seriousness of what the outbreak becomes. Fitzpatrick was never a worthy opponent for Ned, and if this was ever the case, then it would significantly question why Kelly really becomes such a problem for the Victoria Police. The only way that Kelly can be justified, even by his retractors, is to depict him as monolithic in myth as well as his extravagant ability.

Stringybark Creek

After Fitzpatrick came the Stringybark Creek police killings. The later films narrate the killings with little amendment to Kelly's description from his letters. To begin the sequence in Jordan's 2003 *Ned Kelly*, Ned, staring at the stretchers attached to the officers' horses, grimly forebodes: 'they ain't plannin' on takin' prisoners, that's for sure'. So rather than be gunned down like wild dogs, they ambush the police camp. Kelly's first kill at Stringybark was Constable Lonigan. During his 1877 police bashing, he had allegedly told him: 'if I ever kill a man, you'll be the first' (Corfield 2003: 316). In the later films, consistent with his explanation in the letters, cinema-Ned never plans for Lonigan to be his first victim. In Jordan's 2003 film, after Ned shoots the anonymous officer, Dan approaches the corpse to discover its identity: 'Christ, it's Lonigan, Ned. You've killed Lonigan'. In the Jerilderie letter, Kelly excused his accusations of malicious wrongdoing:

> *Lonigan ran some six or seven yards to a battery of logs instead of dropping behind the one he was sitting on, he had just got to the logs and put his head up to take aim when I shot him that instant or he would have shot me as I took him to be Strachan the man who said he would not ask me to stand he would shoot me first like a dog. But it happened to be Lonigan.*
>
> (N. Kelly 1879)

The significant amendment of the Jerilderie letter in Jordan's film, however, is Kelly's admission that Lonigan never 'fired a shot', which does muddle his very argument of 'self defence' somewhat. Ned in the 2003 film only ever kills in 'self-defence', that is, after Lonigan fires the first shot. A shot barely missing Ned's skull is retaliated by one between Lonigan's eyes – an ironic lesson on why one must learn to shoot straight. In these later films, the death of Lonigan is certainly gory, yet perversely satisfying for he is a mean and vicious bully whose comeuppance is deserved. And despite the gang never planning for his death, their unrepentance is apparent when it does come. As Hobsbawm would concur: 'there is just or legitimate killing and unjust, unnecessary and wanton murder; there are honourable and shameful acts. This distinction applies both to the judgement of those who are the potential victims of armed violence' (Hobsbawm 2000: 52).

Sergeant Kennedy

The death of Sergeant Kennedy at Stringybark Creek is a more regretful moment for he is a fair and honest officer. Kennedy has traditionally, and without much deviation, been represented as a first-rate lawman. The famous play *The Cause of the Kellys* (Clow 1919) described Kennedy – in striking contrast to the other officers – as sympathetic and kind: 'Kennedy has a rather pleasant face is inclined to be fair and his beard not so heavy as that of the other three. The other three are dark with heavy black beards' (Clow 1919: 21). In myth, the namesake – Kennedy – is attributed with honest policing. Keneally's fictitious and contemporarily set children's novel, *Ned Kelly and the City of Bees*, as an example, names the caring Sergeant as 'Kennedy' (Keneally 1978). In Southwell's 1919 *The Kelly Gang*, as another example, Kennedy is granted the only moment that comes close to pathos: after goodbyes to his wife and toddler, the following scene has him forebode his epitaph to his superior: 'Do you know, Steele, I feel as if I had parted from my wife and kiddie for the last time.'

The importance of such a scene is not Kennedy's clairvoyance, but an acceptance of his own sacrifice for the outbreak to proceed to its logical conclusion. Kennedy's death gave Kelly the title: 'Outlaw'. While this says much about Kelly's myth, it tends to reveal even more about Kennedy's purpose in the story. In the 1919 film, predicting his own fate, a revenant Kennedy is seemingly informed by the ghost of his past; he foreshadows his demise because he has relived it through the hordes of Kelly entertainment narratives. But more than just this, Kennedy's death allows Ned to regret the mistakes of his own imminent past. In this 1919 film, Ned rushes to Kennedy's aid, ordering Steve, as translated in an intertitle, to 'get some bandages out of the tent – quick!' Ned is desperate here to, literally, stop the bleeding; to save Kennedy's life is his attempt to right this wrong, albeit his own wrong to right. And although his remorse comes too late, he does lament his villainy. This is played out quite blatantly at his Glenrowan capture (to be discussed in the final chapter). But before his own death (and as represented in this film) Stringybark allows Ned to appreciate the enormity of his villainy. The real sadness and tragedy of such a moment is that Kelly does not have the foresight to conclude here. He continues on to Glenrowan to spill more blood – not just the police blood, but the blood of his own gang members – and cause himself even more regret. Keeping in mind the censorship issues hovering over any bushranger production from this time, the sort of empathy of Ned towards Kennedy, as Southwell displayed, was either a bold or a naive choice of direction. The real question, which was surely asked by the censors, was how its pubescent and adolescent filmgoers would interpret Ned's humane reaction towards Kennedy. Does cinema-Ned's empathy romanticise him?

For many, Kelly's killing of Kennedy proves his villainy, as does his decision to write about it. One officer described the Jerilderie letter as 'Kelly's confession' (Lundy 1958: 58). To his defence, historians are of the opinion that Kelly's 'confession' proves his honour and decency to 'do the right thing'. Jones opines that instead of lying, he did the 'right thing', told the truth, and faced the consequences (I. Jones 13 November 2005). To indulge Jones's justification, the films stage Kennedy's demise as a 'fair-fight' – a phrase for which they punctuate. ('It was a fair fight', Kate tells whoever will listen in *The Last Outlaw* (1980).) A hand-held camera and mist effect in *The Last Outlaw* creates a confused atmosphere as further reasoning for why Kelly would have shot an unarmed man. In Jordan's 2003 film, Ned cries at a bullet-riddled Kennedy: 'why didn't you surrender … I wouldn't have shot ya … I'm sorry I shot you'; in Richardson's 1970 film, Kennedy (played by the conservative talkback radio host John Laws) begs 'finish me off man … I can't last much longer'. This dramatised mercy killing goes some way to justify why Kennedy's (widely discussed) autopsy report confirms a fatal shot from close range – assassination style.

Aftermath

In the aftermath of the Stringybark Creek killings, Ned Kelly became a popular news headline. The Melbourne *Argus* sensationally reported:

> *A terrible encounter, almost without parallel in Victoria, has taken place near Mansfield, between the police and four bushrangers. The particulars to hand are but meagre, owing to the intelligence having only been received at Mansfield yesterday evening, but they are of such a character as to show that four most unscrupulous ruffians are at large in the colony, and that no effort must be spared to secure them immediately.*
>
> (23 October 1878: 5)

The Melbourne *Argus* had similar sentiments a few days later:

> *The body was face upwards, and Kennedy's cloak thrown over it. It presented a frightful spectacle. He had been shot through the side of the head, the bullet coming out in front, carrying away part of the face. I believe there are several shots through the body. There was a bullet mark on a tree near where the body was lying. He appears to have been shot whilst running away in the direction taken by Constable McIntyre.*
>
> (1 November 1878: 5)

Readers were so outraged that even Ian Jones had to admit:

> *We are tempted to say that the fuse of rebellion was lit and that the people of the northeast recognised Ned Kelly as their champion. But this is not quite true. There was no immediate support for the Kellys from any but their close friends and relatives. In fact, the first reaction to Stringybark Creek was one of horror and panic.*
>
> (I. Jones 1968: 163–4)

Besides condemning the gang's villainy, the Melbourne *Argus* vehemently criticised the decision to send four inexperienced bushmen to confront Kelly as 'sheer cruelty' (4 November

1878: 6). In remembrance of this historic moment (not just in the history of the Kelly outbreak but the history of Australian policing), a permanent commemorative statue was erected in Mansfield's town centre. For Kelly, Stringybark officially advanced him to the headline of 'Wanted: Dead or Alive'; and, to immortalise the moment, on 23 November 1878, Alfred May produced the very first Kelly news engraving, which appeared on the front cover of *The Australasian Sketcher*. Here the Kelly brothers appear together with the four Stringybark police officers. 'The Bushranging Tragedy' reads the underneath caption. The interesting point about this engraving is the placement of these six characters. Whereas other engravings separated the bushrangers from the police, here they are placed amongst them, surrounding them as they did during the ambush. Gathered by their young and token facial hair, as compared to the mature officers, the identity of the bushrangers is apparent.

Figure 4.1: Alfred May (1878) 23 November. 'The Bushranging Tragedy'. *The Australasian Sketcher*: Front Cover.

Because of Kelly's anonymity, May based this engraving from an 1874 mugshot held by the Victoria Police. This photograph was taken during the felon's Pentridge imprisonment for the sentence of – willingly – receiving a 'borrowed mare'. Kelly's beard growth suggests it was produced in the months before his release, when prisoners were allowed to grow facial hair (McMenomy 2001: 49). This portrait perfectly illustrates the sentiment that Ned was indeed a sinister and threatening-looking felon. But to amplify the villainous myth furthermore, May added the features of eyes drawn closely together and a bandit's moustache. Such an image embellishes the notion that Ned was a delinquent ruffian, spawned from a crooked family. Days after Stringybark, the Melbourne *Argus* heralded:

> *The house of the family has been the rendezvous of thieves and criminals for years past, and indeed has been the centre of a system of crime that almost surpasses belief ... Edward Kelly is notorious as having been arrested in the year 1870 as an accomplice of the notorious Harry Power.*
>
> (13 November 1878: 6)

Recycling this historical news imagery is a scene from Jordan's 2003 film *Ned Kelly*: a hawker selling the latest issue of the Melbourne *Argus* includes a large engraving of the 'villainous'

Figure 4.2: (1874). 'Ned Kelly Mug Shot'. Victorian Police Records. Melbourne: S8369P1.

Australian bushranger. This engraving, prominently canvassed on the side of the hawker's cart, is a complete anomaly to any other perception of Ned viewed in the film. Here he has (literally) become a poster boy: a public spectacle to which the crowd of enthusiastic readers, purchasing their copy of the latest edition, attests. But not a poster boy of 'good' or 'fair' (as in even-handed), this illustration is symbolic of a wider swampland of sensationalist journalism that provokes Ned to respond, dramatically and emotionally in his letters. As the historical Ned Kelly famously wrote in his 1879 Jerilderie letter when he was still at large:

> *I dont think there is a man born could have the patience to suffer it as long as I did or ever allow his blood to get cold while such insults as these were unavenged and yet in every paper that is printed I am called the blackest and coldest blooded murderer ever on record.*

To Kelly's (initial) defence, in the aftermath of Stringybark, however, were the folk ballads. As Seal explains in *Tell 'em I Died Game*: the ballads allowed the sympathisers to defend the shootout as a 'fair fight'. He understands 'Kelly was their Captain' (1878) as the earliest component of the bushranger as a victim of 'official persecution and injustice' (Seal 2002: 41):

> *Now Kennedy, Scanlon and Lonigan in death were lying low,*
> *When Ned amongst them recognised his old and vitreous foe;*
> *Then thoughts came of his mother with a baby at her breast,*
> *And it filled Ned's heart with anger, and the country knows the rest.*

Another tune, circulating shortly after the gunfight, was 'Stringybark Creek'; Seal plaudits it as a 'good-humoured farce, a piece of black comedy that reflects the antipathy of many selectors and bush itinerants towards officialdom in general and the police in particular' (Seal 2002: 45):

> *Then after searching McIntyre, all through the camp*
> *they went and cleared the guns and cartridges and pistols from the tent;*
> *But brave Kelly muttered sadly as he loaded up his gun.*
> *'Oh what a bloody pity the bastard tried to run'.*

Fearing the pervasiveness of the Kelly ballads, the police enforced the Victoria government's decree to ban them. Banning the oral is fraught with great problems – the recorded can be confiscated – but how does one ban something beyond a fixed artefact? One solution was to put a presence where performances would generally occur: pub, social rounds etc. This goes some way to explain the films' regular police presence in the pubs, and to dovetail the police with alcohol as a trope to discredit their professionalism.

Aboriginal 'black' trackers

The Aboriginal 'black' trackers have been another means to discredit the professionalism of the police. The police used the Victorian trackers early into the outbreak (shortly after Stringybark), yet when their searches failed to locate the gang's actual location, the Chief Commissioner, Frederick Standish, felt it pointless to use them any further. During the 1881 Royal Commission, he stated: 'No doubt Trackers can be utilised in following the traces of men on foot, but for this kind of work they are really perfectly useless, because their movements are so slow' (1968: 4). Sadly, no scene of the Victorian trackers remains from *The Story of the Kelly Gang* (1906) despite the programme booklet indicating that Scene Four did feature 'Black Trackers at Work in the Strathbogie Ranges'. The booklet does include a still of the Victorian trackers walking their horses through the scrub. (The Nation Film and Sound Archive holds more stills of the trackers from the film.) The indicators to distinguish the Victorian trackers from the Queenslanders include the Victorian trackers' casual clothes and preferred travel on foot rather than horse.

Evidence of ridicule concerning the Victorian trackers was a cartoon titled, 'Where are the Kellys?' Initially appearing in *The Beechworth Ovens and Murray Advertiser* and later syndicated in the *Sydney Punch*, a tracker, unbeknownst, guides the police party past the cheekily spying gang from behind the gum trees (Figure 4.3). A scene from *The Kelly Gang* (1919) somewhat resembles this *Ovens and Murray Advertiser* illustration of a tracker fruitlessly leading the police party to 'Ned's lookout', without netting the gang. An intertitle transcribes his broken English as he leads the police on their wild goose chase: 'Big pfeller yarraman come alonga here mine tinkit'. Reaching the crest of the hill, an officer looks down to see the gang camped on the other side of the terrain. Supported by such representations, the Victorian trackers did nothing but waste valuable man hours. In the next scene, the gang plan their raid of Jerilderie. The implication: had

WHERE ARE THE KELLYS?

1. Captain Standish and the Victorian police on the *qui vive*. 2. After many weeks, they discover a clue to the whereabouts of the Kelly gang. 3. Who are discovered on the ranges by the light of the moon and the aid of a black tracker, who forthwith makes tracks, followed by the police, to the 4 Awful consternation of the bushrangers.—*Sydney Punch*.

Figure 4.3: (1879) 10 July. 'Where are the Kellys?' *Ovens and Murray Advertiser*: 20.

the tracker been more adroit and correctly led the police to the gang's camp, the outbreak would have ceased much earlier.

The Queensland trackers only appear in the later films. This identifies the fundamental contrast between the two groups of trackers and films: unlike the Victorians' uselessness, the Queenslanders' aptitude and fearlessness made the police seem poltroonery. For this reason, the early films, on account of censorship, do not include the Queenslanders. The Queensland trackers exemplify the incompetency of policing in the colony of Victoria during the nineteenth-century.

Some historical context. After fruitless efforts to capture the Kelly Gang, six Aboriginal 'black' trackers were recruited from Queensland. The Queensland trackers were not officially part of the Kelly hunt until March 1879, which was almost six months after Stringybark. The decision to draft them from Queensland affirmed the general opinion: the Victoria Police were no match for the Kelly Gang. This decision was more embarrassing when the police admitted that in December 1878 Standish had rejected the Queensland government's offer to use their most experienced 'black trackers' (I. Jones 2002: 203). During the 1881 Royal Commission, Standish justified:

> *I confess I was opposed to it, being convinced that, though in a large uninhabited district, where there is a scant population and little or no traffic, the services of the black Trackers, which are chiefly utilized in pursuing and dispersing the native blacks, are of use, it would be very little use in a district where there is a large traffic on all the roads, and where the movements of the outlaws were known to be wonderfully rapid.*
>
> (1968: 4)

The Queensland trackers were widely regarded as the crème de la crème of tracking. The Victorian press reasoned them as to why the gang disappeared for 17 months after their arrival. The Melbourne *Argus*, for example, wrote:

> *It is generally recognised that the fear of the tracking power of the Queensland 'boys' has been a strong deterrent of further crimes by the Gang – indeed the officers of Police know as much. Once they are removed and on the sea journeying homeward, there is little doubt the Gang of outlaws will consider the coast clear and commit a fresh outrage, possibly with loss of life. Information to hand points to the necessity for a replenishment of funds, and as there are many banks unprotected, a fresh crime is easy of committal, and it is felt certain will be committed if once the Gang feel sure they have only to deal with the ordinary Trackers the Victoria Government can command.*
>
> (22 May 1880: 5)

Celebrated in a series of watercolours, produced in 1871 by Samuel Thomas Gill, and commissioned somewhat ironically by Kelly's executioner Sir Redmond Barry, the trackers were immensely skilled at detecting wild and desperate outlaws (Kirsop 1991). Treated with respect and appointed as official 'troopers' of the Queensland Police, they were trained marksmen and given uniforms to identify their fame and rank. (As a point of difference, Victorian trackers were never accepted into the Victoria Police force and indeed they wore their own regular clothes.) During their time in Victoria, however, such esteem was not shown to the Queenslanders. Fearing they would make the Victoria Police look incompetent, the Queenslanders were relegated to the status of 'additional help'. Given on their arrival what Ian Jones terms 'demeaning official names', the troopers became Sambo, Barney, Hero, Jimmy, Johnny and Jacky (I. Jones 2002: 203). Lieutenant O'Connor, who had travelled with the trackers to Benalla, raised concerns about their vulgarity when he publicly declared that the permission given to them in Queensland – to eat the 'bodies of vanquished bushrangers' – would not be tolerated while in Victoria. Such statements seemingly added drama to their myth, as John Molony attests when describing their arrival into Benalla: they were most certainly the 'cause of much speculation' (Molony 2001: 142).

Representing this 'speculation', in *The Last Outlaw* (1980) the trackers are paraded on the Benalla station platform for the inquisitive bystanders and police officials. Dressed in their pristine uniforms of blue tunics and caps, trimmed in red, the trackers bear no resemblance to the style of cavalry uniforms worn by the police officers. Ian Jones's description of the actual trackers recruited from Queensland – 'slim, bright-looking Aboriginals, aged between 17 and 20' – is similar to the trackers from his miniseries (I. Jones 2002: 2003). The physique of the trackers – lean, muscular and handsome – makes some obvious similarities to the representation of the gang by depicting them as a physical match in contrast to the somewhat pyknic Victoria Police officers.

'Let's just hold fire. We really don't know how the traps plan to use them. If they've got any sense they will give the blacks free rein … but would they do that?', wonders Ned in *The Last Outlaw*. And to the gang's boon, no, they do not. The police did not traditionally accompany trackers; in actuality, their inferior horsemanship only slowed them down. However, because Captain Standish took the view that any credit given to the trackers would be credit deflected from the police he insisted that they be accompanied at all times, despite the negative ramifications this caused to the reputation of the police. Depicting this, in Richardson's *Ned Kelly*, the adroit trackers locate the gang's vicinity. 'Kellys very near … we go catch them', asks one enthusiastically, to which the cowardly officer responds with instructions to leave. A few years after Richardson's film, the children's book, *Bold Ned Kelly*, also used this episode to mock the lily-livered officers: 'The police were afraid to meet the Kellys in the bush after Stringybark and decided to return to their base' (Johnson 1977: 36). Yet, as historical engravings illustrate, the cowardice of the police, in comparison to the trackers, is not just a contemporary representation: one 1881 engraving by Julian Ashton depicts a group of officers sitting stationary on their horses, while a Queensland tracker eagerly gallops in search of Kelly (Figure 4.4).

Figure 4.4: Julian Ashton (1881) June 18. 'The Black Tracker'. *The Australasian Sketcher*: Supplement Edition.

The 1879 theatre play *Catching the Kellys* – advertised in the Melbourne *Argus* as a 'farce' (29 March 1879), and a 'sketch' in the *Brisbane Courier* (28 August 1879) – represented the trackers and the Kellys as friends – not foes. Veronica Kelly in the *Annotated Calendar of Plays* gives a detailed synopsis:

> *A Queensland bush sheriff escorts two blacktrackers to 'catch the Kellys'. The trooper party wander aimlessly and are captured by the Gang. The play from here seems to reach a new level of absurdness. The Kellys then drink themselves into a stupor, are revealed to be amateur Police in disguise, and the Black Trackers turn out to be Irish.*
>
> (V. Kelly 1997: 79)

The Last Outlaw does represent the Kellys to have great admiration for the Queenslanders. Operating as a go-between for the gang, sympathiser and Kelly cousin, Tom Lloyd, marvels 'not just Black Trackers ... they are fighting men. They can use a gun. They keep the cannibals down along the Palm River'. Ned's sister Maggie echoes his infatuation by fetishising their 'magical powers': 'They put on a show. Do you know that one picked where a man had touched a slip rail ... by the specs of salt from the sweat from the palm of his hand'. *The Last Outlaw* (1980) is not alone in its reverence towards the Queenslanders. In Tony Richardson's

1970 film, Joe Byrne's fear of the trackers – 'they will probably catch us in our beds' – provokes Ned to send Caitlyn home: 'You can't stay here love … it's not safe here. It's not safe anymore. The black trackers can trace us anywhere now. On the run, in the bush, it's no place for you'.

The problem of the Victoria Police was their disdain for Aboriginal peoples. Mocking such times, in the comedy *Ned* (2003), Governor Sinclair is completely contemptuous and ignorant towards his recruited Chinese tracker who he initially confuses as Aboriginal. When he does come face-to-face with an 'authentic' Aboriginal he queries: 'Why is he burnt … he looks nothing like the last one'. Once Ned is captured, the tracker – no longer needed – is blindfolded, bound and used as the target for a shooting game. Just as disturbing, the 1977 comic *The Iron Outlaw and Steele Sheila* illustrates an Aboriginal tracker chained and led like a savage beast. In the background, a line of indigenous porters carry boxes of goods for the white superhero outlaws (Figure 4.5) (Rutherford 28 February 1971: 9). Written by Graeme Rutherford and illustrated by Gregor MacAlpine (28 February 1971), this sketch focused on Ned Kelly and his voluptuous offsider, Dawn Papadopolis (a council typist) cum Steele Sheila, as they drive around the country in an orange GT striped and mag wheeled FJ Holden. Appearing weekly in Melbourne's *Sunday Observer*, this became one of the most popular tabloid strips of the 1970s.

Figure 4.5: Graeme Rutherford and Gregor MacAlpine (1971) 1 July. 'The Iron Outlaw and Steel Sheila'. *Sunday Observer*: 24.

'I have yet to read an account of the Kellys that has managed to integrate the trackers into its narrative', Routt writes in discussion of *The Story of the Kelly Gang* (1906) (Bertrand and Routt 2007: 81). Indeed there are accounts that do satisfactorily document the trackers involvement in the hunt: Gary Presland's *For God's Sake, Send the Trackers* is one such example (Presland 1998). Yet, Routt is not entirely wrong. Speaking broadly about commentary on the Kelly outbreak, the trackers have been a terribly aborted feature of the historicisation. The outbreak, traditionally, has been a duel of whiteness fought between the Victoria Police and Kelly Gang. And despite the trackers' involvement at various stages of the hunt, they only make fleeting appearances in the story. In *The Last Outlaw* (1980), for instance, the Queensland trackers are on the Special Police Train to the Glenrowan siege with the police; however, once the battle begins, they are not seen again. Jordan's 2003 film includes no more than one brief shot of the trackers. But, to accuse the films of historical neglect would ignore history-Kelly's accusation of the Victoria Police as his sole enemy. The films – especially the later films – are interested in narrating the outbreak as Kelly documented it in his Jerilderie letter.

Aboriginal peoples and the Irish certainly had much in common, especially their oppression and their attitude towards the Crown. Like the Irish, the British settlers treated Aboriginal communities quite appallingly during colonisation. So with this in mind the idea of Aboriginal trackers hired to negate Kelly's rebellion against British hegemony becomes a somewhat hysterical prospect for they really had no grudge to bear. What Kelly threatened to destroy was the very class system that had impoverished, slaughtered and fragmented Indigenous Australia. Yet despite their mutual sentiment, the gang still feared the trackers enough to backtrack all the way to the snowfields – a climate too arctic for their pursuers to endure.

In the Jerilderie letter, Kelly declares the Victoria Police as his true enemy. There he accuses them of conducting many unlawful raids in his family's shanty:

> *I heard how the Police used to be blowing that they would not ask me to stand; they would shoot me first and then cry surrender. And how they used to rush into the house and upset all the milk dishes, break tins of eggs, empty the flour out of the bags onto the ground, and even the meat out of the cask and destroy all the provisions and shove the girls in front of them into the rooms like dogs, so as if anyone was there they would shoot the girls first.*

John McQuilton argues that such condemnation of police persecution – as documented in the Jerilderie letter – was echoed by the witness accounts, deposed during the 1881 Royal Commission on the outbreak. In reflection, it surely is hard to regard the police all that positively, particularly considering the incredibly unconvincing testimony that Constable Fitzpatrick submitted to begin the saga in which he accused Kelly of attempted murder.

The Jerilderie letter

More than any other historical account, Kelly's Jerilderie letter, together with its early genesis in the Cameron letter, gave him a voice to respond directly to the public vitriol regarding his ambush and killing of three police officers at Stringybark Creek. Written when still at large, the manifesto is punctuated with threats and warnings: 'I am a widows [*sic*] son outlawed and my orders must be obeyed'. In Richardson's 1970 film, he declares 'words are very loud, if only you could use them … suppose I write a letter'. Representing Kelly as someone to possess the intellect and manner to assemble at his log table and write is a key to mythologising him as literate; and, the letter as evidence of his social banditry. Yet, rather than critically challenge his letter's content, the films faithfully, and with no amendment, adapt them. ('Ned wrote it so is must be true' is their general attitude.) As a point of likeness, compare Kelly's explanation of the police ambush in the Jerilderie letter ('We thought it best to try and bail those up take their firearms and ammunition and horses and we could stand a chance with the rest' (N. Kelly 1879)) to his orders in *The Last Outlaw* (1980) ('Bail them up, take their guns and horses off them and send them back from where they came'). 'Every dilemma here – and there are a couple – is not a dilemma at all, but merely a matter of making an obvious choice', writes Routt on Jordan's film (Routt 2003c: 17).

Kelly's 5200-word manifesto first appeared as a complete 'unedited' document in Max Brown's *Australian Son* (1948, 1956) for which he titled it the 'Jerilderie Letter'. Newspapers had initially published edited excerpts before this time. To ensure that their felonious and illiterate depiction of Kelly is not muddled, the letters are never referenced in any of the early films; cinema-Ned's pack-mentality in these films allows him to be consistent with the condemnations that were once placed on the Kelly Gang. As a point of difference, the later films treat the writing as the achievement of an inspiring and well-read spokesman. The Kelly represented here is someone who is politically engaged and willing to sacrifice his freedom for the rights of his folks. The language of the letter(s) (letters as in plural for it also includes Kelly's earlier missive written as an open letter addressed to Donald Cameron MLA) must not be overlooked, for their style and prose directly informs the language of the Kelly tradition which define the later films.

Sensitivities concerning the representation of the police are the obvious reasons for why Kelly's letters are absent from any of the early films; to include his description of them as violent thugs, surely, would have guaranteed their censorship. In these films, the police do not use the procrustean methods Kelly accused them of – his 1877 Benalla public bashing or innocence of the Fitzpatrick attempted murder charge are completely ignored. In such films, cinema-Ned is visibly in attendance during the Fitzpatrick incident, another point disputed in the letter. Other historical accounts swear that Kelly was, without a doubt, Fitzpatrick's gunman: the surviving Stringybark officer, Constable McIntyre, states in his memoirs that Kelly did shoot Fitzpatrick, despite not being in attendance himself (McIntyre 1902: 12).

The historian John McQuilton trumpets the Jerilderie letter as proof that Kelly was a nineteenth-century social bandit, 'a rare thing indeed' (McQuilton 1979: 209). The letter maps out the obvious social banditry dimensions of the outbreak, which the later films incorporate to project cinema-Ned as a social bandit. Beyond narrating the tried-and-true battle of the Crown versus the Kellys, the later films cover the collective rural discontent demonstrated by those in support of Kelly's rebellion. Persuaded by the Jerilderie letter's convincing and compelling argument for why Kelly should be placed under the umbrella of 'social bandit', they narrate the Stringybark Creek saga almost verbatim as Kelly wrote it. This in and of itself has provoked considerable criticism: Jill Kitson on *The Last Outlaw* (1980), for example, damned its resistance to delve any further than Kelly's rhetoric. ('At the same time, there is weighty evidence that Kelly was a cold-blooded murderer, something which the script played down disquietingly' (Kitson 1981: 56).) More than other artefacts, Kelly's letters become his voice from beyond the grave; his DNA says Peter Carey, who wrote his Kelly novel as homage (in language, style and rhythm) to the Jerilderie letter's vernacular. It is told in the first person, and locates the outbreak in Kelly's poor Irish selector background.

Composition

While the diary of Superintendent Sadleir, held at the State Library of Victoria, speaks of the Jerilderie letter as not 'unexpected', the later films regard it as something truly amazing (Sadleir 1913): 'Maybe you have made a bigger impact than you think ... people are saying you don't act like other bushrangers', sympathiser Tom Lloyd marvels in *The Last Outlaw* (1980). In its correct context, however, letter writing during the nineteenth-century was not such a big deal. Kelly at the age of 15 wrote to Sergeant James Babington while in gaol. In his tiresome appeal, he concluded with claims of unfair persecution: 'Everyone looks on me like a black snake' (N. Kelly 1870). Writing certainly gave Kelly a platform to direct his contempt and outrage towards those who he felt had victimised his family. In the Cameron missive, he lamented:

> *This sort of cruelty and disgraceful conduct to my brothers and sisters who had no protection, coupled with the conviction of my Mother and those innocent men certainly made my blood boil as I don't think there is a man born could have the patience to suffer what I did. They were not satisfied with frightening and insulting my sisters night and day, and destroying their provisions and lagging my Mother with an infant baby and those innocent men, but should follow me and my brother, who was innocent of having anything to do with any stolen horses, into the wilds where he had been quietly digging and doing well, neither molesting or interfering with anyone.*
> (N. Kelly 1878)

Entirely convinced, and thus unwilling to challenge Kelly's word, Ian Jones marvels at how the Jerilderie letter reveals the 'fire, passion, the reality of the past as it lived in Ned Kelly' (I. Jones and Tomasetti 1968: 77). Composed at the height of the outbreak, the Jerilderie letter bestows an eerie and dramatic insight into the bushranger's psyche; it responds directly to the scathing press that labelled him as 'vicious and bloodthirsty'. 'A premeditated and atrocious crime has been perpetrated by a gang of ruffians', the Melbourne *Argus* opined (29 October 1878: 5). To the member for West Bourke in the Victorian Legislative Assembly, Donald Cameron MLA, Kelly wrote:

> *Dear Sir,*
>
> *Take no offence if I take the opportunity of writing a few lines to you, wherein I wish to state a few remarks concerning the case of Trooper Fitzpatrick against Mrs Kelly, W. Skillion and W. Williamson, and to state the facts of the case to you.*
>
> (N. Kelly 1878)

Written in red ink on foolscap, it totals 22 pages, and was composed as a missive that Cameron could read to the parliament. While duplications of the letter have been preserved, the whereabouts of the original is not known. Dramatising Cameron's dismissal of the letter, Ned in *The Last Outlaw* (1980) reads from an actual Melbourne *Argus* report:

> *The leader of the gang has written a voluminous letter to a member of the Legislative Assembly, in which he relates his history, and alleges that his mother and other friends, who are at the present in gaol for assaulting a constable, have been wronged by the police. He asks for no mercy for himself, but demands that justice shall be done to his friends, and threatens to do diabolical acts if his request is not complied with. The letter is evidently written for the purpose of exciting public sympathy.*
>
> (27 December 1878: 3)

Responding with outrage:

> *When was a politician interested in any more than his own pumped up sense of power? They sit in their precious monument at the top of Bourke Street, playing parliament in a grand English manner. What do they know, what do they care about poor country people in far away places. Here's a letter, laugh at it, throw it in the waste paper basket and down to the club for a drink, while the mother of 12 wastes away in gaol for something she never done. What are we gonna do to make them listen?*

Determined to see his version of events circulated (in his own words), Kelly dictated another letter. Depicting the same events of the outbreak, its penmanship is eloquently superior to the Cameron missive, and longer, covering 56 pages. Gang member Joe Byrne (writer of many Kelly ballads) surely had more involvement in its composition. To recognise its brash humour, one scene from Jordan's 2003 film has the police officials try (unsuccessfully) to withhold their chuckles as the Victorian Premier, Graham Berry, seemingly unaware of its wit, reads them aloud its most uproarious paragraph:

> *[M]y brothers and sisters and my mother not to be pitied also who has no alternative only to put up with the brutal and cowardly conduct of a parcel of big ugly fat-necked wombat headed big bellied magpie legged narrow hipped splaw-footed sons of Irish Bailiffs or English landlords which is better known as Officers of Justice or Victorian Police.*

Not premeditated in Jordan's 2003 film, the letter's composition is the result of a hostage – during the gang's raid of the New South Wales Bank – accusing them of being 'a bunch of *common* criminals'. Infuriated that his martyrdom is mistaken for thuggee, cinema-Ned growls at his gang, 'if we act like common criminals that's exactly what they will call us'. He continues to the hostages:

> *My mother is rotting away in a prison cell because of the lies of a policeman named Fitzpatrick. She's an innocent woman and so are these boys here. My Irish brethren have been unlawfully imprisoned and blacklisted from their selections. How do you expect me to behave other than stand up against this treatment ... if I can beg your patience, this is my statement to the Premier of Victoria, Graham Berry, and you are my witnesses ... Joe get together your pen and paper.*

The image of Ned dictating his words – a monologue of sorts – as he stands amongst his hostages, certainly denotes the letter as a declaration of 'community' grievances; its composition becomes a manifesto of public unity. The document, which Ned produces, and the language that Berry reads to his officers may be bombastic, quixotic and hysterical but nobody – not even Berry's gentrified brethren – could fairly define it as 'common'. A reason for Kelly's outbreak (echoed by the films) was to demand change: feed his impoverished community, and institute what would later be interpreted as a Republic of North-Eastern Victoria. There is nothing 'common' about this as there is nothing 'common' about the image of this so-called bush rogue sitting in Richardson's 1970 film at a log table, somewhere in the Wombat Ranges, composing his letter. Ned, in this film, scrawls his words as Maggie, seated next to him, reads aloud his sentiment of Irish nationalism:

> *What would people say if they saw a strapping big lump of an Irishman shepherding sheep for fifteen bob a week or tailing turkeys in Tallarook ranges for a smile from Julia, or even begging his tucker? They would say he ought to be ashamed of himself and tar and feather him.*

Ned here is seemingly composing the Cameron letter, despite his dialogue being pulled from the more eloquent Jerilderie missive. Most certainly, the film blurs, to some degree, the letters to ensure that Kelly is represented as a rousing wordsmith. Unbeknownst at the time of the 1970 and 1980 films, however, the depiction of Kelly penning the letters was factually wrong. To their defence, these films, like any historicisation, can only mine the 'available' facts. So, rather than dismiss them for historical inaccuracy, such inaccuracies document how history continues to amend and rewrite the Kelly story. Graphological research has since confirmed

Joe Byrne as the true penman of the letters. This is why in Jordan's 2003 *Ned Kelly*, Joe transcribes as Ned stands before him dictating. Yet, to ensure that such an image does not suggest Kelly as illiterate, Joe's penmanship is merely a means of convenience; Ned's dictation is an amusing and theatrical performance that requires him to be free of pen and paper.

The very notion of Kelly having the skill to produce such eloquent writing – now accepted without too much debate – for many decades was nothing more than a fantastical notion. Historical accounts commonly depicted him as a dim-witted bumpkin. Professor Richard Berry's famous 1926 Medical School lecture, at the University of Melbourne, compared the developmental size of Kelly's brain to that of a 13-year-old juvenile (R. L. Jones 2007: 120). The Melbourne *Argus* regularly discussed Ned's 'illiteracy' by reporting (on one occasion anyway) that 'neither of the Kellys can write' (13 November 1878). During the outbreak, Constable Thomas McIntyre, in his manuscript, also remarked on Kelly's inability to compose the Jerilderie letter himself (McIntyre 1902: 59). Another manuscript, written after the outbreak, and allegedly by a surviving Dan Kelly (seemingly from the ashes of his incineration inside the Glenrowan Inn), acknowledges Joe as the only member capable of such diction:

> *I ought to say that he was the only member of the gang who could write at all. We others were so far from penmen, that if obliged to write, we had to scrawl our letters in the shape of print. Longhand was unknown to us.*
>
> (Pratt 1911: 12)

Supporting Kelly's education is Richardson depicting him writing his letter in the company of Kate – she bears witness to her brother's literacy. Following from this, Jones's *The Last Outlaw* (1980) portrays the letter as Kelly's masterstroke; handing it over – a close-up of the letter is used for emphasis – he forcefully insists: 'this is very important to me Mr Irving … fifty-six pages of my life, do you understand?' Jones certainly had an intimate knowledge of the letter: in 1968, Keith Harrison claimed to have possession of the original copy, stored in his fireplace. But, with neither the State Library of Victoria nor National Library in Canberra believing it to be the actual manuscript, nor willing to take possession, Jones became its unofficial custodian, and official presider, until its authentication was finally completed in 1985 (I. Jones 2006). In November 2000, the State Library of Victoria uploaded a digitised version onto its website. Within five days it was boasting to having scored over 80 000 hits (I. Jones 2000: 33).

Republican Ned

While the letter never mentioned the r-word, it is often championed as Kelly's declaration for a republic:

> *But as soon as I am dead they will be heels up in the muroo. there will be no more police required they will be sacked and supplanted by soldiers on low pay in the towns and special constables made of some of the farmers to make up for this double pay and expense. It will*

pay the Government to give those people who are suffering innocence, justice and liberty. If not I will be compelled to show some colonial strategem which will open the eyes of not only the Victorian Police and inhabitants but also the whole British Army and no doubt they will acknowledge their hounds were barking at the wrong stump.

(N. Kelly 1879)

Wary of branding Kelly a republican, John McQuilton writes how 'republicans', especially during the nineteenth-century, were indeed:

associated with revolutions led by educated and organized men who are highly aware of the political process ... or, at the very least, an awareness of ways to manipulate a political structure to achieve reform.

(McQuilton 1979: 168)

Contrary to Jones, who is of the opinion that Kelly was a publicly acknowledged republican, McQuilton concludes: 'to have expected Ned Kelly to have formulated an organised political structure for his republic is ludicrous. The man had neither the education nor political experience for such sophisticated planning' (McQuilton 1979: 169). Persuaded by Jones's somewhat munificent lionising are the later films illuminating Kelly as literate, a great leader, strategic and inspiring – and republican. Aware, however, that revolutionaries are not necessarily republicans, in the later films, the reward for Kelly's revolution is a republic; this is what the sympathisers want and this is what his letters are interpreted to declare.

It is intriguing that not until Jones presented his explosive paper, 'A New View of Ned Kelly', at the 1967 Wangaratta symposium, did anyone publicly discuss Kelly as such (I. Jones 1968). Even the pro-republican newspaper, *The Bulletin* (first published in January 1880) described Kelly in no uncertain terms as 'synonymous with terror' – not republicanism (3 July 1880: 9). Mark McKenna's book *The Captive Republic* on Australia's troubles to remove itself from the British Commonwealth struggles to write Kelly into the republican vernacular:

the least interesting of Republicans and the least typical. His simplistic, aggressive and shallow rhetoric may fit the mould of the stereotypical Republican hero but there were few Republican heroes in Australia. Unlike Kelly, Australian Republicans were politically active individuals who eschewed political traditions and the story of their role as Australian political culture is an exploration of the intellectual history of pro-federation Australia.

(McKenna 1996: 123)

Presenting a similar representation, Kelly's impetus – in the early films – is to attack those partisan to the Crown: gentrified hostages, bank tellers and police dressed in British Cavalry uniforms. 'There will be no more police required', Kelly foreboded in the Jerilderie letter. Regardless of the early films making no mention of the letter, it does seem to directly inform their representation of his sheer anarchism, instead of political republicanism.

In direct resistance to such a representation, however, Jones's *Last Outlaw* (1980), in one critical scene, portrays Kelly composing his highly discussed, but never located, declaration: 'The Republic of North-Eastern Victoria'. While Jones understands the declaration to have been printed in the 'form of handbills', in this miniseries cinema-Ned scrawls on the type of paper seemingly identical to the Jerilderie paper. In 1962, Leonard Radic, claiming to have witnessed the declaration, came forth detailing its 'old fashioned block type and quaint, mock legalistic language' (I. Jones 2002: 224). In *The Last Outlaw* (1980), apart from Ned writing the words, 'The Republic of North-Eastern Victoria', none of the manifesto's content is revealed, in any form (Figure 4.6). Again, like Maggie in Richardson's 1970 film, or the hostages in Jordan's 2003 film, in the 1980 miniseries the sympathisers gather to bear witness to the composing of the manifesto. Yet, unlike the ubiquitousness of his letters, all one can do with the declaration is take the word of his sympathisers (and Jones). Furthermore, like the Jerilderie letter's composition in Jordan's film of Ned dictating to Joe while standing amongst his hostages, in *The Last Outlaw* the sympathisers surround him in another display of community harmony.

Figure 4.6: The Declaration of North-Eastern Victoria (*The Last Outlaw*, 1980).

The declaration is one trope to demonstrate Kelly's republicanism; another is a constant hammering of his republican cause during his emotive speeches to his hostages and sympathisers. As a case in point, in Richardson's 1970 film he implores:

> *[W]e have to fight for our own colour ... the green flag of Ireland and if we declare war on the whole English world and claim this as our land and our law then our oppression and suffering will perish like the frost melting on the green lawns of Ireland. Friends let's drink to it, to our own republic – to the republic of Victoria.*

So on they march, until of course Glenrowan becomes too much to endure; any idea of a republic is eclipsed by the stark lament of what could have been, which is to overthrow the British hegemony. British hegemony is represented in the comedies in the manner of clueless autocrats: Sir John in *Reckless Kelly* (1993), staring at the silhouette of a kangaroo, boorishly asks, 'Is it a rodent?' Such representations further support Graham Seal's argument that the English are traditionally lampooned as stuffy, pompous and unable to endure Australia's bucolic outdoors (Seal 1990). The Briton Francis Adams in 1891 conceded that in Australia 'the bush is the heart of the country, the real Australian Australia, and it is with the Bushman that the final fate of the nation and race will lie ... the English cannot thrive far from the sea' (Adams 1968: 196–197). A symptom of this myth, indeed, is a seedier impression of Australia as an infested swampland of the convict rogue; the folk song, 'The Pommy's Lament' is such an example:

> *All you on emigration bent,*
> *With home and England discontent,*
> *Come listen to my sad lament*
> *About the bush of Australia.*
> *My convicts, they were always drunk,*
> *And kept me in a mighty funk,*
> *Says I to meself as to bed I sunk,*
> *I wish I were out of Australia.*

(Manifold 1964: 31)

Sending Sinclair a boatload of convicts to kill, the Queen in *Ned* (2003) epitomises the representation of Australia as a demonic wasteland. In further allegiance to the British Empire, Sinclair, standing before a mammoth British flag and dressed in his crimson red Cavalry uniform, tells jokes to his troopers about the 'potato-eaters'. ('How many Irish men does it take to change a light bulb? Ten. One to hold the bulb and nine to rotate the ladder'.) *Reckless Kelly* (1993) – each member of the Kelly clan represents a different marginalised racial demographic (Italian, Greek, Chinese, Aboriginal etc.) – unabashedly promotes Ned to the role of the republican spokesman, as did Yahoo Serious during the film's promotion when he championed Prime Minister Paul Keating's push for a republic of the Australian Commonwealth (Crompton 12 April 1993: 35). The blatant example of republicanism in this

Figure 4.7: Thomas Carrington (1879). 'The Outlaw Premier' in Ian Jones and Thomas Carrington's *The Last Stand*: 10.

film is Sir John striding into his office to discover Ned tearing the Union Jack off the Australian flag that is pinned above his desk. 'That's the British flag', he bellows, to which Ned coolly replies, 'Well, take it back to Britain then'. Surely intended to amplify Kelly's resolute republicanism, historically he has been portrayed as someone audacious enough to encroach a dignitary's office. For example, an 1879 Thomas Carrington engraving – 'The Outlaw Premier, No. 2' – depicts Ned and Dan inside (British-born) Berry's vacant office. Ned in the Liberal Premier's chair is seated alongside a vandalised plaque that has the 'Honourable G Berry' cheekily replaced with the 'Honourable E Kelly'. To accompany this caricature, the caption reads:

> *I'll burst up the banks and squatters better than the Chief Secretary himself. I'll put my hand into the public purse in an easy, accessible and peaceful manner; and now I'll cancel all the Government Gazette notices against me and my mates.*
>
> (I. Jones and Carrington 2003: 10)

As this chapter has discussed, when Kelly is conceived as a republican he becomes a political figure who challenges and threatens the political order. Invoking Irish republican ideals, he attempts to confront the injustice and oppression experienced by his family and forefathers. Representative of this, Kelly in the later films demonstrates the importance of

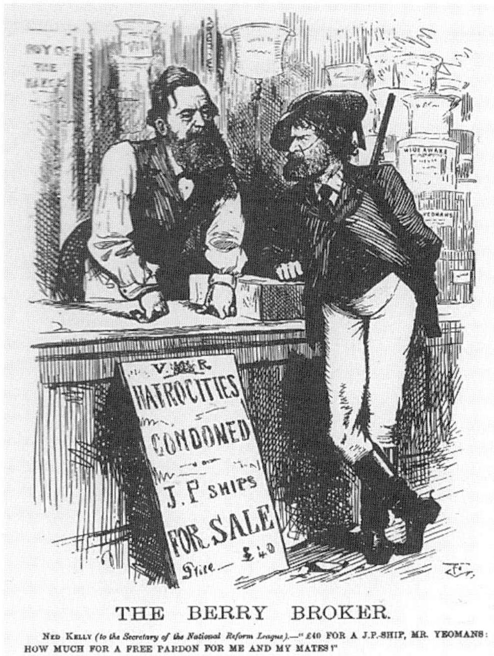

Figure 4.8: Thomas Carrington (1879) 16 January. 'The Berry Broker'. *The Melbourne Punch*.

his Irish heritage as he hopes to achieve economic and political equality by distributing government money to the poor and, of course, attacking corrupt officialdom. However, to only speak about Kelly and his Irish heritage ignores his wider body of support, which sustained him during the outbreak. Whereas Kelly in the early films is only supported by his immediate family, the representation in the later films closely resembles John McQuilton who interprets the outbreak as a united 'protest against oppression and poverty, a cry for vengeance on the rich and oppressors, a vague dream of some curb on them, a righting of individual wrongs' (McQuilton, 1979: 4). Kelly's wider network of support will be the focus of the following chapter.

Chapter 5

The Noble Bandit: Irish Sympathy and Other Sympathy

As Eric Hobsbawm argues, 'the worst thing that can happen to a bandit is to be cut off from his local sources of supply, for then he is genuinely forced to rob and steal, that is to steal from his people, and may therefore become a criminal who may be denounced' (Hobsbawm 1959: 17). No such behaviour is required in the later films: the pay off for cinema-Ned's benevolence and martyrdom is aid from many racially spread communities, including the Irish, Chinese and Aboriginal peoples. Cinema-Ned's 'mad-Irish' identity certainly allows him to justify the outrage as a political rebellion, intended to establish a Republic of North-Eastern Victoria. Invoking Irish republican ideals, Ned proves that living by his noble robber code is quite liberating. As an Irishman, he attempts to erode the injustice and oppression experienced by his family and forefathers.

From England's Robin Hood to India's Phoolan Devi, the noble robber is an outlaw who benefits from community support by accepting a code of higher principles: 'his role is that of the champion, the righter of wrongs, the bringer of justice and social equality'. Hobsbawm elaborates:

> *The noble robber is the most famous and universally popular type of bandit, the most common hero of ballad and song in theory, though scarcely in practise ... His role is that of the champion, the righter of wrongs, the bringer of justice and social equity. His relation with the peasants is that of total solidarity and identity.*
>
> (Hobsbawm 2000: 46–47)

He further plaudits Robin Hood as 'what all peasant bandits should be' for they always plunder in moderation and only kill in self-defence (Hobsbawm 2000: 46). Gathering there is something quite ludicrous about using a fictional figure as the benchmark for a real-life outlaw, Robin Hood is how many outlaws would like to be imagined. Also, it is how many historians want to remember Ned Kelly, as Ian Jones opines:

> *A Robin Hood-like figure survived: good-looking, brave, a fine horseman and bushman and a crack shot, devoted to his mother and sisters, a man who treated all women with courtesy, who stole from the rich to give to the poor, who dressed himself in his enemies' uniforms to outwit them. Most of all a man who stood against the police persecutors of his family and was driven to outlawry when he defended his sister against the advances of a drunken constable.*
>
> (I. Jones 2002: 338)

Bail up

Since the early commodification of Kelly's visual tradition, he has become a symbol of the noble robber myth. An 1880 penny-dreadful cover, for instance, depicts Kelly riding down the steps donned in his helmet, in a stance closely resembling an engraving of his 'Victorian cousin, Dick Turpin' (James and Smith 1998: 14). Plays perpetuated the myth of 'Kelly the Highway Robber'; *Fleeced or the Vultures of the Bush or the Vultures of the Wombat Ranges* (first performed on 16 November 1878) is said to have consisted almost entirely of Ned performing elaborate scenes of 'highway robbery' (V. Kelly 1997: 73). Even witnesses during the criminal trial deposed:

> *Daniel Kelly, Joseph Byrne, and Stephen Hart formed an organised Gang of armed highway robbers, under the leadership of the said Edward Kelly, and during the said period were the cause of much terror to the law-abiding and peaceable inhabitants of the said northern bailiwick.*
> (20 September 1880: 7)

Exciting tales about Kelly's highway robbery exploits give further historical weight to his popular representation as a gentleman robber. Paradoxically, however, there is absolutely no categorical evidence to confirm that his gang committed any highway robbery, at any point, 'during' the outbreak. As a 'Wanted Outlaw', Kelly only robbed banks. Yet narrativising the myth that he did actually, before the outbreak and in his salad days, partake in highway robbery, *The Last Outlaw* (1980) details an adolescent (but never delinquent) Ned accompanying the infamous gentlemanly highway robber Harry Power on a series of bail ups. Working as an apprentice, Ned never actively participates in any of the robberies. Camouflaged by the bushes, he witnesses a firsthand demonstration of the noble robber criteria: never rob the poor and always use violence in moderation. Neglecting to mention the fact that Kelly was charged with two counts of highway robbery (on 5 May 1870), Jones overlooks Kelly's darker reality to safeguard his prime-time television special from receiving an AO (Adults Only) classification. This miniseries was, cheekily, promoted as accurate in 'every detail'.

Playing up history-Kelly's highway robber myth, *The Story of the Kelly Gang* (1906) portrays the gang – viciously and brutally – loot the van of the poor Scottish hawker, James 'Sandy' Gloster. In actuality, this incident occurred at Younghusband's Station, in the lead up to the Euroa bank raid. Before Gloster arrived, the gang had already bailed up the inhabitants of the station; unsuspectingly he found himself at the outlaws' mercy. For Kelly buffs, the name James 'Sandy' Gloster is most certainly familiar: he deposed during the criminal trial as to how Kelly had threatened to 'put a bullet in his head' (10 August 1880: 7). As understood by the Police Commissioner, John Sadleir, Gloster was the only hostage at Younghusband's Station to openly oppose the gang: 'of all these was only one man, a hawker named Gloster, who made any show of resistance' (Sadleir 1913: 202). In her Special Commentary, to accompany the restored DVD version of the 1906 film, Sally Jackson marvels at Gloster's slapstick gesticulations (Jackson and Shirley 2007). This sequence migrates directly from the theatre, the industry most associated with the Taits: the camera's stationary and far-ranged position – to allow characters to enter and depart the shot, as they would a stage – photographs this unnamed actor's rousing performance. However, the gang's rough rather than rough-house behaviour towards Gloster and his junior partner (portraying Frank Beecroft) is somewhat troubling: holding him at gunpoint, they aggressively pilfer his fancy clothes, cigars and liquor, along with other supplies. The actual historical reason as to why the gang stole Gloster's clothes was to look respectable for their Euroa bank robbery. In spite of this point (not being implied by this film), the gang take great pleasure in threatening and manhandling Gloster.

Affirming their reputation as a bunch of thugs, in *The Story of the Kelly Gang* (1906) and *The Glenrowan Affair* (1951), a bank teller during the Jerilderie band raid is threatened by Ned to 'do as I say'. Receiving no applause from his hostages, and not demonstrating the sort of benevolence that would warrant any 'support' in all of the early films, Ned is given an ultimatum from his so-called sympathisers: 'pay us or we talk'. Here the gang are marginalised from their own socio-demographic: 'Margins on the margin'. Yet, instead of being concerned, they relish the role of the outcast bush rogues. *The Story of the Kelly Gang*'s (1906) programme booklet explains how the Euroa bank robbery ends with the gang mate Steve Hart riding, not towards, but away from the hostages with a 'bag of money' (J. Tait and Tait 1906: 2). Promoting this villainous representation, as part of its marketing campaign, the theatrical poster for *The Kelly Gang* (1919) dramatically reads 'the terror of the whole continent fighting his last lone fight'. Consistent with this period of the Hollywood western's global permeation, the early Kelly films enthusiastically celebrate wicked acts of violence. Such films, in content and promotion, had great fun decorating the villainous ways of the outlaw baddie.

Because the later films are more concentrated on story, and cinema-Ned's identity as a somewhat conventional Irish hero, his behaviour towards the hostages is almost incomparable. *The Last Outlaw* (1980), for instance, depicts Gloster as a supporter of the gang's cause: generously he donates them his swanky clothes and use of his hawker's van for their daring Euroa bank raid. Moreover, a striking contrast to *The Glenrowan Affair*'s (1951) Jerilderie bank raid is this same sequence reworked in Jordan's 2003 film. Here Ned grabs Steve Hart by the scruff of the neck and insists that he return the hostage's 'damn watch … I'm not gonna tell ya again kid'. Apart from the occasional resister, hostages in such films behave more like sympathisers and accordingly treat Ned as some kind of colonial hero. For instance, the hostages during the bank 'bail up' in *Ned* (2003) adoringly flock around him. Muffy to conclude the sequence shyly asks 'will you allow me but one kiss'. Attempting to grant her wish, Ned masked by his helmet, accidentally dongs her on the head. (Legend says that hostages were so enthralled to see the 'real' Kelly that during bushranger Jack Bradshaw's 1880 robbery of the Quirindi Bank, one hostage naively asked whether he was indeed Ned Kelly.)

Lampooning the idea of history-Kelly, as a revered celebrity, in *Reckless Kelly* (1993), Ned aptly changes his career of outlawry to a career of show business; travelling to Hollywood he stars in the 'B' Picture 'The Christian Cowboy', as a partisan of God, who 'cleans up the rottenest town in the West' for the Sisters of Mercy. Throughout the outbreak, history-Kelly's stagy exhibitionism and impromptu speeches during his bank raids created quite a buzz. Jones believes this to have significantly provided the gang with a 'public platform – a chance to display themselves as highwayman heroes such as Australia never had seen' (I. Jones 2002: 160). Sticking with this showman trope, to begin their bank robbery in *Ned* (2003), the gang perform a choreographed dance to the grooved-up rap-tune 'Bushrangers with Attitude'; outside, a street stall includes an assortment of paraphernalia branded by the slogan: 'I was robbed by the Kelly Gang'. In *Reckless Kelly* (1993), after Ned's bank robbery cum depository into the account of 'anyone who cannot afford to repay their home loans' (where he introduces himself as 'the Kelly Gang'), the film cuts to a television news report, featuring 'city locals' praising the bushranger for 'lowering interest rates and raising the standard of living'. Staging a similar capitalist critique in Richardson's 1970 film, upon his horse (doubling as a suitable stage), he lectures to his Euroa Bank hostages about his noble deeds, and the need to document them in a letter:

> *Ladies and gentlemen, before you go there is something that I'd like to say, the newspapers have called me a murderer but my conscious is as clear as the snow in Peru. I have never murdered anyone, I have killed police in a fair fight, but if I had been defenceless they would have shot me down like a dog. I was outlawed without cause while seeking justice for my mother and if I got that justice I will cry a go, but if I do not I will seek revenge while God gives me strength to pull the trigger. I have written a letter explaining all of this.*

Irishness

A cause of Ned Kelly's outrage, and staple of his noble bandit representation, is his Irish identity. There is indeed some historical truth to his representation as Diaspora Irish. Though the historical Kelly did not speak Gaelic, he was immersed in a community heavily populated by Irish Catholic selectors. For history-Kelly, there was no escaping his Irish heritage: his father Red was transported from Tipperary to Van Diemen's Land in 1841 for stealing pigs; his mother Ellen Quinn was born in Antrim, Ireland and came to Australia in 1841 with her parents. The offspring of an oppressed race, the Irish-Catholics were treated disdainfully, and with great suspicion. Defined as a 'special class', they formed Australia's first white minority and 'from the outset, the Irish in Australia saw themselves as a doubly colonised people' (Hughes 2003: 181). Even John McQuilton, who argues against the tendency to over-stress Kelly's Irish element, 'because it is so obvious', cannot ignore its significance (McQuilton 1979: 188). Through his Irish identity, cinema-Ned becomes more sympathetic and empathetic, which is why the early films felt it necessary to make him an ocker Aussie to ensure the censors would not accuse them of romanticism. The later films, which are all about romanticisation, exemplify Patrick O'Farrell's comments regarding a more new age Irish stereotype. In *The Irish in Australia*, he writes:

> *The idea of being 'Irish' has undergone a remarkable recent transformation from being identified, historically, with poverty, ignorance, low social and occupational status, sectarian*

> *Catholicism, drunkenness, disorderly behaviour. It has recently become a fashionable asset, representing charm, sociability and conviviality, mild social radicalism, fun and entertainment, possessing some of the essential ingredients of the popular Australian self-image. By 1995 it was politically correct to call the Irish delightful.*
>
> (O'Farrell 2000: 330)

As Manning Clark understands: 'so Ned came to man's estate a divided man – aware, too, that such acts against the men who had condemned many a blooming Irishman to a life of tyranny were not crimes' (Clark 1968: 17). Cassandra Pybus makes similar claims by arguing that Irish outlaws are culturally identified as oppressed 'Irish political heroes' (Pybus 2002: 31). In Jordan's film, Ned voices this sentiment sardonically:

> DAN: *You're just gonna keep running, aren't you? They'll catch you eventually or shoot you down. Did you know they pardoned Frank Gardiner in New South Wales?*
>
> NED: *On condition he left the colony.*
>
> DAN: *He gave himself in.*
>
> NED: *He wasn't an Irishman.*

These later films represent Kelly as an intelligent and charming proud Irish son who, of course, still enjoys a whiskey and dance. More than just cinema-Ned's own Irish identity, these films are fittingly set within an iconographic Irish miasma, which further bolsters some sympathy towards his dire situation.

Ireland?

In spite of the North-East of Victoria's reasonably hot and dry climate, the overcast, cold and wet landscape of the later films suggests the boggy terrain of Ireland. A montage early in Richardson's 1970 *Ned Kelly*, for instance, showcases the hungry countryside as Ned travels home from his stint in the Pentridge prison. As images illustrate an impoverished and fruitless milieu, Ned's outbreak is more justified for somebody needs to make a stand and 'feed the poor'. Social banditry, Hobsbawm writes, becomes 'epidemic in times of pauperization and economic crisis' (Hobsbawm 2000: 26). Representative of this is also Jordan's 2003 *Ned Kelly*, which presents an equally dire and destitute environment – overshadowed by ominous clouds and cold weather. William Routt describes this film's visuals as drenched in colours of black, tan and grey – 'predominantly the colour of dirt, dust, rocks, wood and mud' (Routt 2003c: 12). The season of winter is the backdrop for these films: in *The Last Outlaw* (1980), the Kellys end their evening by gathering around the fire and listening to Ned read excerpts from the novel *Lorna Doone*. (This English novel narrates the struggles of a poor family of selectors trying to resist the persecution of procrustean police.) On this blubbery melodramatic moment, Jill Kitson writes:

> *Willow-pattern china stood on the polished dresser and on the warmly-varnished kitchen table; pictures hung neatly on the wall, and in the flickering light of the open fire, the clean, well-mannered, loving family ate their Irish stew, listened to Ned reading* Lorna Doone, *and withstood the blows of a cruel world.*
>
> (Kitson 1981: 57)

A direct contrast, however, is the sunny, vigorous and most-suitable-for-farming representation of the Victorian landscape in the early films. Thick, vigorous shrubbery and sun surrounds the Kelly homestead in *When the Kellys Rode* (1934). Open fires are not required for warmth – the healthy landscape gives no apparent justification for outlawry. In images that evoke scenery of the Australian Heidelberg School (Frederick McCubbin, Tom Roberts), the vast landscape of bushland becomes an enthralling and visual splendour; the bushrangers are dwarfed by the long shots that punctuate the 1934 film – anonymous specks on the horizon.[1]

Figure 5.1: The sunny terrain (*When the Kellys Rode*, 1934).

In the later movies, as a further point of contrast, the landscape is cruel and hard. Despite its tranquil beauty, it is not an easy milieu to endure. In Jordan's 2003 film, the gang (in a relatively short time) become a dishevelled mess in the miasmic terrain: matted hair, dirty and sunburnt by the shifting environment, they are barely recognisable from their normal stylish selves. These kinds of images certainly paint a sympathetic as well as heroic portrait of Kelly, whose quest for justice is crippled by the brutal landscape. The landscape, however, allows the films to establish another binary concerning the gang's duel with the police: whereas cinema-Ned is respectful of the indigenous milieu, the police in their searches recklessly contaminate and destroy the environment. Poisoning watering holes in Richardson's 1970 film, in Jordan's film they recklessly start a bushfire to 'smoke out' the gang.

Folk ballads

Beyond just the seemingly Irish milieu, however, is the use of Irish folk ballads. Early into Jordan's 2003 *Ned Kelly*, Aaron Sherritt uses music to shield Ned from a standoff with the contingent of police officers: 'This one is a request for Ned Kelly', he hollers as the assortment of musical troupes erupt into a spirited rendition of 'Kesh Jig'. Dancing amongst his fellow patrons, Ned is rhythmically placed in harmony with his community. And amongst his folks on the dance floor, he cheekily grins at Constable Lonigan – a cheeky grin of victory. 'Nerve of the bloody knacker', the Constable retorts from the side. 'Look at him. Acts as if he owns the joint'. Despite this paradox of Lonigan (in reality) being Irish, such ancestry is ignored in favour of giving the Victoria Police the label of 'racist British thug'. Irish music, as a boundary between the sympathisers and resisters, is a staple amplified throughout the tradition. However, during the bans on the bushranging films, directors and exhibitors needed to ensure the ballads were not used in any way to pity the outlaws. During *The Story of the Kelly Gang*'s (1906) Australian premiere tour, for example, Sydney Monk sung popular ballads 'prior' to the feature's screening, but not 'during' its presentation (24 January 1907: 8). In Melbourne, a narrator announced lines from the back of the auditorium, during the Athenaeum Hall performances (24 January 1907: 8).

Like Kelly's Irish brogue (to be discussed shortly), the balladry also frames him within the oral tradition of the Irish-rebel-hero. William Brennan is one obvious example; the opening lines of 'Brennan on the Moor' seem nascent to the sentiment echoed later in many of the Kelly ballads:

It's of a fearless highwayman a story I will tell,
His name was William Brennan and in Ireland he did dwell,
And upon the Libbery mountains he commenced his wild career
Where many a wealthy gentleman before him shook with fear.

(Seal 2002: 17)

According to Graham Seal, this Brennan ballad foregrounds the sentiment of 'stressing the outlaw's bravery, courtesy, and his standing as a friend to the poor' (2002: 17). And as would be the case for popular music, a century later, the subgenre of 'outlaw country' became a more modernised version of the folk ballad. In 1968, Bob Dylan wrote and recorded an entire album inspired by the Texan outlaw titled, *John Wesley Harding* [*sic*] (1968). (This was Dylan's misspelling of Hardin, and pronunciation, on the title track.) Not surprisingly, Richardson had originally wanted Dylan to record his Kelly soundtrack. In an interview he declared how 'Dylan, like Jagger, can present the human reality of the rebel, the justifiably angry rebel that the historical Kelly really was' (Rawlins 2 August 1969: 9). Unable to obtain the services of Dylan – who would go on to score one of the great bandit films *Pat Garrett & Billy the Kid* (Peckinpah 1973) – American country singers, Waylon Jennings and Kris Kristofferson instead performed a number of folk ballads as written for the film by Shel Silverstein.

Regardless as to whether it be the police at the pub in Jordan's film, or Lillian Roxon deeming the 1970 soundtrack as 'appalling', Kelly ballads have continued to offend (Roxon 21 June 1970). George Wilson Hall's 1878 book, *The Kelly Gang or, the Outlaws of the Wombat Ranges* even prefaces its readers to the affront that awaits:

> *We have limited our extracts to the most harmless portions to be selected from the mass of leprous distilments of the composer's perverted genius, such as it is, feeling confident that the majority of readers will join our estimate of the wretched and mischievous production, inductively judging what the character must be of the lines we have withheld from publication, as being outside the limits of decency and order. The following lines form a portion of a bad parody on 'The Bould Sojer Boy'; this sample will be enough of the song to judge by. It refers, of course, to the Kelly Gang.*
>
> (G. W. Hall 1878: 60)

McQuilton writes how 'young toughs had taken to singing pro-Kelly ballads in 1879 to taunt the police' (1979: 144). Performance as a public statement of social protest, the sentiments of the Kelly ballads were reverberating around the country: in 1879, Hobart theatre broadsheets included the Kelly songs, 'Ballad of the Kelly Gang' and 'Sticking up of the Euroa Bank'; in this same year, *The Mansfield Guardian* distributed a pamphlet featuring the lyrics to four Kelly ballads (Seal 2002: 3). The circulation of these ballads does prove Kelly's heroisation amidst his outlawry; however, posthumously, Kelly's oral musical tradition gained great momentum. In 1897, a successful magic lantern tour featured Joe Watson singing folk songs as Kelly magic lantern slides were shown (Fahey 1975: 3). Elizabeth Hartrick in her Ph.D. thesis on the magic lantern phenomenon in Australia and New Zealand outlines the common songs, canticles, recitations, hymns and comic narratives that would have been performed at such presentations: 'Singing aroused feelings of community and enjoyment, and the message of salvation was conveyed through "modern" hymns and songs accompanied on the screen with text slides and illustrations' (Hartrick 2003: 100, 199). An interesting continuum here is Tony Richardson's 1970 film. Utilising the folk ballads to narrate important background information, and explain on-screen action, the songs take on an important narrative device by substituting for dialogue – to explain some necessary back-story as well as excusing Ned's more questionable behaviour. Jennings, paradoxically, sings 'Ned Kelly ain't never done wrong' over images of Ned chasing an unarmed Sergeant Kennedy through the woods at Stringybark Creek.

'The Wild Colonial Boy'

Graham Seal asserts how the ballads echo 'the man's own words, and in the words of the people who saw him as something more than a common criminal' (Seal 2002: 10). The gang member Joe Byrne – described in Tim Burstall's 'Man in Iron' screenplay as a 'poet' – was said to have written many Kelly ballads including 'Stringybark Creek', 'Euroa', 'Jerilderie' and 'The Ballad of the Kelly Gang' (Seal 2002: 6). In *The Last Outlaw* (1980), Joe performs a rendition of his 'Ballad of the Kelly Gang'; the claps from the intimate gathering keep rhythm:

It was when they robbed Euroa bank you said they'd be run down
But now they've robbed another one that's in Jerilderie town
That's in Jerilderie town, my boys, and we're here to take their part
And shout again 'Long may they reign – the Kellys, Byrne and Hart'.

At the conclusion of this performance, Ned praises its overriding theme of Irish-Australian rebellion: 'you wrote a grand old song there … a proud old Irish tune in the words of a trueborn colonial son'. Jones identifies this ballad as a reworking of 'Wearing of the Green', a tune that dealt specifically with the theme of Irish oppression. Dubbed by a sympathiser as 'Hymns of Triumph', it was 'sung to a clapping of hands and stamping of feet'; the performance from *The Last Outlaw* (1980) seems to mirror such a description (I. Jones 2002: 201).

As with *The Last Outlaw*, in Richardson's 1970 film, folk ballads are sung inside a pub, or an enclosed space – sometimes a sympathiser's home – where alcohol is plentiful. Before this 1970 film, Australian troubadour Glen Tomasetti had been attached to the Kelly lore by interleaving a number of Kelly ballads into Jones's presentation of his paper, 'Kelly – The Folk Hero', at the 1968 Wangaratta Kelly symposium (I. Jones and Tomasetti 1968: 74–103). In the 1970 film, the patrons, spread throughout the pub, stop their chitchat to hear Tomasetti's quite poignant rendition of 'She Moved through the Fair'. In another scene, in another pub, Jagger sings, 'The Wild Colonial Boy', which is the only ballad that he performs – albeit in two very different renditions. For the first time, he sings it a cappella. Spitting the words with rebellious panache into the face of Constable Fitzpatrick (played by *A Stone in the*

Bush director Martyn Sanderson), who enters mid-way into the performance, the gathering demonstrate their anti-authoritative unity by joining in the chorus:

Come, all my hearties! We'll range the mountain side;
Together we will plunder, together we will ride.
We'll scour along the valleys and gallop o'er the plains;
We scorn to live in slavery bowed down with iron chains.

This song's title ('The Wild Colonial Boy') was in fact a famous idiom for outlaws who enjoyed the 'help of a sympathetic network of friends, commonly known as the "bush telegraph"' (Engwerda, Cotter and Anderson 2000: 50). John Molony understands 'The Wild Colonial Boy' to be Kelly's most beloved ballad (Molony 2001: 176). In Richardson's 1970 film, Ned sings it for a second time, inside the Glenrowan Inn, as the gang and hostages wait for the Special Police Train to arrive. Different from his earlier a cappella, this one – accompanied by musical troupes and chorus from the hostages – is fast, rough-house and raucous. A colonial rock performance one might say. To delineate these different editions, Helen O'Shea posits they:

> *convey characteristics associated with stereotypes of the Irish ... the first is the melancholy soprano wail that throughout the film gives voice to emotions of pain, loss, heartbreak, longing, and romantic love. The second is the lively, vigorous sound of Irish dance music that accompanies scenes of earthy celebration, pranks and high spirits ... these twin musical representations of Irishness, also employed in the music tracks to the Ned Kelly films, have a long history.*
> (O'Shea 2005: 38–39)

Most certainly they do. The version of the ballad used in Richardson's 1970 film is about the Tasmanian-born Jack Doolan; like Kelly he never ventured to Ireland, despite his ancestry. Graham Seal claims 'The Wild Colonial Boy' to be anthemic of the Irish spirit:

> *In the Anglophone context, it is also the Irish element that imparts a distinctive connotation of political dissent. The fact that 'The Wild Colonial Boy' was often sung to the tune of the 'The Wearing of the Green', a melodic icon of Irish revolt, is a further indication of the importance of the 'Celtic connection'*
> (Seal 1993: 169)

No narrative captures the essence of Hobsbawm's social banditry code better than the 'The Wild Colonial Boy' (Seal 1996: 37). In his paper, 'The Wild Colonial Boy Rides Again', Seal deconstructs it to mirror Hobsbawm's nine enumerations of the noble robber:

The 'Wild Colonial Boy' scores well in various versions of his song:
1) He is a member of a nationality that is widely represented as oppressed.
2) He is brave and defiant.

3) *He robs the wealthy squatters or in some versions, a judge. In an American/Irish version he is said to have 'helped the poor'.*
4) *He is adept at disguise, eluding pursuers and escaping from tricky situations.*
5) *He dies game.*
6) *While not betrayed in a direct sense, many versions of the song have him being deserted by his cowardly companions in the ultimate moment of need.*

> *The 'Wild Colonial Boy' therefore scores six out of nine, for those who like numbers. But as well as these considerations, it is arguably the very clearly articulated revolt of the Wild Colonial Boy against the powers of authority and law that make the song, in all variants, so internationally appealing.*
>
> (Seal 1993: 168)

'The Wild Colonial Boy' continuum is globally ubiquitous indeed. Appearing in many different accompaniments, despite the Irish-American version celebrating the Colonial Boy as a Robin Hood figure – robbing the rich to help the poor – in Australia, the ballad became popular during the gold rush era of the 1850s and 1860s. Perhaps more suitable than any other example, it articulates how every outlaw would rather 'die game' than surrender (Seal 1996: 37). Hence, the Kelly Gang members Steve and Dan chose death in a suicide pact at Glenrowan rather than capitulation. ('"I'll fight but I won't surrender", said the Wild Colonial Boy'.)

'Moreton Bay'

In Jordan's 2003 edition, the folk tune 'Moreton Bay' (also known as the 'Convicts Lament on the Death of Captain Logan' and 'The Convict's Arrival') echoes the sentiment of the 'Wild Colonial Boy'. Seal describes it as a song about 'the suffering of a transported Irishman', narrating the story of an unnamed colonial rebel-killer of the tyrant Captain Logan (Seal 2002: 90). This ballad had such a penetrating influence on Kelly's lore that many, such as Jack Bradshaw, recognise it as a 'Kelly Ballad', despite it being in circulation since the 1830s, some 50 years before Kelly's hanging (Manifold 1964: 27). In the Jerilderie letter, Kelly not only poached one of 'Moreton Bay's lines – 'many a blooming Irish man rather than subdue to the Saxon yoke were flogged to death and bravely died in servile chains' – but further routed the ballad's lyrical and rhythmic style. This is why the two accompany one another so fittingly in performance. On Graham Seal's musical LP record, *Game as Ned Kelly* (1980), the letter is read to the accompaniment of Irish bagpipes playing 'Moreton Bay' (Seal 1980). Discussing the song's hold on Kelly's missive, Seal explained:

> *Poorly educated, poorly represented in Parliament, and just plain poor, the Kellys, and many like them, had no other means of expressing their anger than through the inherited images and clichés of Irish nationalism.*
>
> (Seal 2002: 90)

In Jordan's 2003 film, Bernard Fanning – lead singer of the now defunct Australian rock band Powderfinger – performs a mournful rendition of 'Moreton Bay'. Both the Jerilderie letter and it narrate a similar story of Irish nationalism and oppression.

The metamorphosis of Kelly ballads is found in more contemporary genres of musical protest, including rock 'n' roll. The casting of Fanning in Jordan's film is evidence of this, as is Midnight Oil's 'If Ned Kelly were King' (Midnight Oil 1981) and The Whitlam's 'Kate Kelly' (Whitlams 2002). Furthermore, beyond direct dovetails to the bushranger himself, the comedies also include contemporary 'outlaw' songs to demonstrate the universality of Kelly, and his identity as an international outlaw rebel. *Reckless Kelly*'s 'I Fought the Law' and 'Wild Thing' (1993), or *Ned*'s 'The Fun Lovin' Criminals' and 'Damn It Feels Good to be a Gangsta' (2003) are not songs specifically written about Ned Kelly, but in the context of his modern day anti-authoritarian image, they suitably celebrate him as part of the (global) tradition of noble robbers.

Non-Anglophones

One way to represent Kelly's benevolence and wider support is to depict (and exaggerate) his relationship with non-Anglophones: Chinese and Aboriginal peoples. The Chinese and Aboriginal peoples are the non-Anglophone 'others' that have become more integral to the Kelly story over the last few decades. Before this time, they appear as either Aboriginal 'black' trackers or pesky hostages (as the Chinese hostage epitomises in *The Story of the Kelly Gang* (1906)). Until the 1970s, the Aboriginal peoples and Chinese were only seldom depicted as collegial towards Kelly. There were a few satirical plays during the nineteenth-century, but none with the intention to seriously challenge the popular view of Kelly's attitudes towards non-Anglophones. The Kelly story and Kelly sympathisers were exclusively white. Only in the past few decades has this changed; only since white Australia has rethought its reliance and heritage of non-white communities and ancestry. To now think of Ned Kelly as accepting of non-whites is to regard white Australia's colonial relationship with non-whites more positively. By foregrounding cinema-Ned's relationship with the Chinese and Aboriginal peoples, across the films as well as broader cultural and historical commentaries, the remainder of this chapter will track his transformation into the racially benevolent noble bandit.

Chinese

The Chinese stand as important allies for Ned Kelly in the later films. Through these films, nineteenth-century colonial history is provided a more generous evaluation of non-white racial prejudices. Not to suggest that the Chinese community members are accepted into the fore of white settler rituals, their placement, nevertheless, is more porous than narrativised by most historians. Here they interact with whites, socialise with the Kelly Gang members (their association is through the experience of being outcasts) and share a resistance to British hegemony. Before this more recent cycle, however, Kelly was commonly represented as a staunchly xenophobic fellow. During World War II, a Kelly folk ballad – 'Ned Kelly was a Gentleman' – was reworded as propaganda to encourage young men to enlist.

And perhaps now in Australia we'd have millions trained with him,
All laughing with a vengeance at the little yellow men.
If Ned and such guerrillas were here with us today,
The Japs would not be prowling round New Guinea and Milne Bay.
Since Ned went over the border there has been many a change,
Yet we may adopt his tactics around the Owen Stanley Range.
Poor Ned, he was a gentleman, but never understood:
We want men of such mettle now to stem the yellow flood.

(Seal 2005: 144)

The folk song *The Ballad of the Kelly Gang* – supposedly written by Joe Byrne – also treats the Chinese rather brutally:

They bailed up all the servants and placed them in a room,
Saying, 'Do as we command you, or death will be your doom',
The Chinaman cook, 'no savvy' cried, not knowing what to fear,
But they brought him to his senses with a lift under the ear.

(Seal 2002: 9)

Popular during the outbreak, this tune featured on theatre broadside sheets in 1879 (Seal 2002: 7). A sound recording – held by the State Library of Victoria – includes the version of the ballad that folk singer Joe Watson sang on magic lantern tours in 1897 (Watson 1976). It intriguingly evinces minimal modification since its 1879 circulation – a rare occurrence for the oral. Including some new phrases, the 'Chinaman' verse survives erosion:

Sure they bailed up all the servants and locked them in a room
Saying, do as we do bid you, or death will be your doom.
A Chinaman cook 'no savvy' cried, not knowing what to fear,
But they brought him to his senses with a lifting under the ear.

(Fahey 1975: 5)

Demonstrated by the books – *Australian Bush Ballads* (D. Stewart and Keesing 1955) and *Ballads and Songs Collected by the Missouri Folklore Society* (Belden 1940) – Chinese hostages are often exploited, beaten and bullied in bandit lore. In *The Story of the Kelly Gang* (1906), as an example, Ned threatens a Chinese hostage at gunpoint (Figure 5.2).

Figure 5.2: Chinese hostage stands centre (*The Story of the Kelly Gang*, 1906).

Historical examples demonstrating Kelly's contempt towards the Chinese are plentiful: they 'buy white women' he declares of them in his Jerilderie letter (N. Kelly 1879); Francis Hare during the 1881 Kelly Royal Commission accused Kelly of exploiting local Chinese storekeepers:

> *The Chinaman said, 'No fear; Kelly up at Buckland; get supplies from Chinamen'. He said, 'They come down frequently from the mountains with pack horses and take their supplies. But do you not tell Policemen about it. If you do, Chinaman's store get burnt, my garden destroyed and everything, you are not to say a word about it'.*
>
> (1968: 81)

Similar accusations circulated about Kelly's resentment towards the Beechworth Chinese before the outbreak actually began: on 10 October 1869, Ah Fook accused Ned Kelly of assault; however, due to his 'inconsistent testimony' (which probably had to do with his poor English) all charges against him were dismissed (Corfield 2003: 7). Jones claims that

Kelly had helped Harry Power bail up Ah Fook in a stagecoach robbery some six weeks earlier (I. Jones 2002: 37).

Hobsbawm considers racial prejudice as a ritual connected – almost exclusively – with anti-social avengers: those who inflict acts of 'ultra-violence' on racial minorities. He writes:

> *Several of the best-known examples of ultra-violence are associated with particularly humiliated and inferior groups (e.g. the coloured in societies of white racism), or with the even more galling situation of minorities oppressed by majorities.*
>
> (Hobsbawm 2000: 70)

In *The Last Outlaw* (1980), Ah Fook, or any Chinese for that matter, is not a victim of Harry Power's highway robberies. *The Last Outlaw*, like all the later films, represents Kelly to have a collegially peaceful and friendly repartee with the Chinese, even though such a representation is not consistent in written texts. For example, the children's book *Ned, A Leg End,* published a few years after the release of *The Last Outlaw*, shows the haphazard bushranger 'accidentally' exploding a number of fireworks in Ah Fook's store (Ferrier 1984). Following its lead from the Jerilderie letter, Peter Carey's 2000 novel, *The True History of the Kelly Gang*, has Ned declare the Irish as a race ethically superior to that of the Chinese:

> *Perhaps if I were a Chinaman I might have had the sense to betray Harry Power without no shame I cannot say but we Irish was raised to revile the traitors' name.*
>
> (Carey 2000: 195)

Jones, in dispute, reckons that there is no historical evidence to suggest that Kelly had anything but an affable rapport with the Chinese. This is certainly the sentiment of the later films. In Jordan's 2003 film, the Chinese and members of the Kelly Gang rub shoulders at the local tavern. Contrary to the many historical engravings representing Chinese and alcohol as incompatible, here the Chinese are relaxed, jocular and peaceful. Historical reports certainly confirm the concerns of the police that the Chinese were 'dangerous' allies of the Kelly Gang. Evidence of this was the placement of three Chinese detectives in heavily populated Chinese communities; 100 copies of Kelly reward posters, in the 'Chinese' language, were also drafted.[2] According to Corfield's translation, they stated:

> *Last October three Policemen were murdered near Mansfield by four bushrangers who are still at large and have since plundered two banks. A reward of £8000 will be given to any Chinese who gives information to the Police by which the offenders are captured – or £2000 if only one of them is found – for it is known that they obtain food from the Chinese on the Upper Murray River and along Woolshed Creek.*
>
> (Corfield 2003: 104)

There is no doubt that the police persecution against the Chinese immigrants mirrored that of the Irish selectors: the 1882 Australian theatre sketch, 'Drift', narrates the hysterical farce of 'Black Ned' forming a gang with some Chinese who trick and deceive some rich British squatters (V. Kelly 1997: 110). Despite its ridiculous plot, it demonstrates how outcast minorities require a bit of trickery in order to survive in the capitalist/consumer market.

Taking this idea further, a Chinese merchant in *The Last Outlaw* (1980) endeavours to trick the gang during a gold exchange transaction. Smelling honey inside his gold-measuring funnel, Ned shrugs off the merchant's attempted deceit: 'Cunning old beggar', he chuckles. Hobsbawm opines how sly black-market business operators (as represented by this merchant) are among banditry's essential characters. Defining them as 'middlemen', Hobsbawm suggests that this role requires shopkeepers, innkeepers and merchants to link bandits with larger networks of 'legitimate' commerce:

> *Like Pancho Villa, they must have at least one friendly hacienda across the mountain which will take, or arrange to sell, livestock without asking awkward questions.*
>
> (Hobsbawm 2000: 93)

As consistent throughout all of the later films, cinema-Ned is reliant on the Chinese to operate. In *The Last Outlaw* (1980) and Jordan's *Ned Kelly* (2003), the gang are close with the Chinese groups because of Joe Byrne's fluency in Cantonese. In *The Last Outlaw* (1980), Ned marvels at Joe's incredible talent: 'I've never heard anything like it … when did you learn to speak Chinese'. In reply, Joe explains:

> *There was a Chinese camp across the creek from home. I was always hanging around there. I just picked up the language. It is like a song you keep hearing. You don't try and learn it, but you do.*

John Molony in his book *Ned Kelly* – shares *The Last Outlaw*'s (1980) explanation for Byrne's bilingualism:

> *Nearby to the Byrne home on the Woolshed there was a Chinese camp to which the quick-witted Joe often went and listened, fascinated, to their tongue, so that in time he acquired a modest mastery of its mysteries, and won the trust of those who had learnt to fear the white man since the riots on the Buckland in the golden days.*
>
> (Molony 2001: 65)

Joe's relationship with the Chinese was so well-known that a local officer had once demeaned him as 'half a Chinaman' (I. Jones 1992: 24).

> *In this atmosphere the Byrne children grew up to accept the gently industrious Cantonese as neighbours, with their coolie hats, dungarees and sandals made of pieces of plank fitted with leather throngs.*
>
> (I. Jones 1992: 7)

A renowned opium smoker, Joe Byrne's habit was dependent on remaining collegial with the Chinese drug traders. (Not that opium consumption in Kelly's age was a seedy and underground industry. Considered a 'Chinese indulgence', which relates to British imperialism in China, the Australian colonies allowed its sale and use. Intervention would occur only when reports confirmed a high dependency of white gentry (Oldis 2008).) Ian Jones identifies Byrne's dependency in his history books – *The Fatal Friendship* (I. Jones 1992: 24) and *A Short Life* (I. Jones 2002: 87) – but ignores it in *The Last Outlaw* (1980), as do the other films. For the films to depict Joe as drug fuelled would have severely compromised their stalwart depiction of him. He appears as a composed and disciplined lieutenant to Ned, free of any vices that he cannot control. His only real vice, however, is freewheeling philandering, as one Chinese character mocks in Jordan's 2003 film – in Cantonese – over a drink in the tavern: 'you know, the Chinese say you should only have one true love in your life. Otherwise you are no better than a mangy dog or loose woman'. Nevertheless, Chinese women are not immune to Joe's Don Juan allure either: while holed up at Julia Cook's cattle farm, he seductively entices her (Chinese) maid to a back-scrub as he enjoys a smoke while relaxing in the bath.

An important confidant for Ned, Joe offers sound council when required. In Harry Southwell's silent *The Kelly Gang* (1919), Joe (transcribed by the intertitle) advises Ned: 'You and Dan better join Byrne and Hart in the Ranges'. Echoing such sentiments in Gregor Jordan's 2003 film – 'you and Dan ought to clear out for a day or two … just to be safe. God willing it will all blow over'. And the place where they indeed find refuge is on the Chinese gold fields. In Richardson's 1970 film, as a point of difference, Ned's Chinese sympathisers are noticeably westernised, which does have some historical truth: in the Victorian colony many Chinese did saturate themselves in western culture. Carole Woods (*Beechworth: A Titan's Field*) understands Chinese to have dressed in western clothing as a prerequisite for attending Anglican churches (Woods 1985: 69). In order to read the Bible, many learnt English. The Chinese sympathisers in Richardson's 1970 *Ned Kelly* are noticeably dressed in western style fashion. They speak English also. (This is the only film where Chinese do/can speak English.) Not to suggest, however, that Richardson's concern is (entirely) their Anglican influence: their English (let's assume they also can speak some dialect of the Chinese languages) is a cheap way to avoid subtitles, which was not a popular devise in 1970. More significantly though, in this film there are no cultural divisions between the Irish and Chinese; they all rebel as one and speak together (in the same language) as one. They also dress in a similar style; apparelled in fashionable waistcoats, hats and scarfs, they mimic Ned's/Jagger's own fashion style.

The Chinese sympathisers in Tony Richardson's *Ned Kelly* (1970) and *The Last Outlaw* (1980) play a crucial role during the Glenrowan siege. In Richardson's feature, Ned forcibly instructs his two Chinese sympathisers – representing the actual sympathisers Ah Ping and Ah Soon:

> *Now understand this: take the rockets down to the station and wait behind there until the train is wrecked … and then fire the rockets. Tom Lloyd and all our loyal friends*

> *and supporters are waiting in the hills. That's the signal for them to join us. Do you understand?*

Assigning them the role of artillerymen makes them auxiliary gang members of Ned's quest to annihilate the Victoria Police. Their involvement here demonstrates Ned's faith to entrust them with such a role at Glenrowan, despite the irony of them igniting the firecrackers prematurely. Following a more accurate representation, however, in *The Last Outlaw* (1980) the Chinese sympathisers have no more involvement beyond handing over some firecrackers, free of charge. Here, Ned's overzealous cousin Jack Lloyd is the one to prematurely explode the firecrackers.

Aboriginal peoples

As with the Chinese, it is a struggle to locate positive representations of the Aboriginal peoples in the nineteenth-century. In the 1829 play, *The Bushrangers*, 'the BLACKS' 'assume menacing attitudes'; are incapable of adopting civilised behaviour; and 'perform a *rude* dance in which they go spinning round and round and throwing their arms about in an extravagant manner and singing' (Burn 1829: 30). The play's premise: the creation of a 'civilised' Australian society depended on the migrated principles of the white settlers, like Englishman Matthew Brady. To end the play, Brady escapes his convict detention and saves a woman from rape (Burn 1974). During the epoch of Kelly's outbreak, the Aboriginal peoples were popularised as 'creatures' to be held in mortal fear; commonly they were 'monsterised' as 'Bunyips', which *The Beechworth Ovens and Murray Advertiser* defines as 'wild black fellow' (13 November 1874: 1). When humanised they were mostly stripped of their 'Aboriginality'. For example, in the 1920s (year not known) 120-page penny dime - *Ned Kelly: A Tale of Trooper and Bushranger* – Ned's Aboriginal friend closely resembles a Hollywood Red Indian (Hayter n.d.).

Despite no historical account identifying any Aboriginal as a registered-by-the-police sympathiser, John McQuilton understands Kelly to have a lifelong bond with Aborigines: 'regularly camped on the banks of the creek near the Kelly shanty. Ned Kelly's admiration of the skills of the black trackers during the outbreak probably stemmed from this boyhood contact' (McQuilton 1979: 75). Making assertions that the Aboriginal peoples, also, held Kelly in high esteem is the book *But Now We Want the Land Back*, which mythologises Kelly as a positive figure among the indigenous camps (Middleton 1977: 121). Seldom represented beyond the Aboriginal 'black' trackers before the 1970s, since this time the Aboriginal peoples have enjoyed more active friendships with Ned in popular culture. Thomas Kenneally's novel *Ned Kelly and the City of Bees*, for instance, includes an Aboriginal character who nurses Ned back to health (Keneally 1978). A staple of Aboriginal peoples as ministering angels emerged during this time with other examples including the bushranger film *Mad Dog Morgan* (Phillipe Mora 1976) and the children's book *Ned, A Leg End* (Ferrier 1984).

Cinema-Ned since the 1970s has mostly enjoyed a good-natured relationship with the Aboriginal peoples – not that any historical evidence exists to support this; his relationship is based purely on myth. *Reckless Kelly* (1993), as an example, includes Aborigines as part of the extended Kelly family dating back 40 000 years to the first Kelly outlaw, Awaba Kelly. Ned further acknowledges his Aboriginal uncle Dan Kelly as the finest – now retired – bank robber to have ever lived. The film, topically, is dovetailed to debate from its time of production for the landmark *Mabo v Queensland* High Court of Australia decision, which rejected the doctrine of *terra nullius* (ie land belonging to no one) and recognised native title in Australia, was just a year earlier.

At the time of its release, others were also publishing similar mythology about Kelly's 'historical' relationship with the Aboriginal peoples; a series of academic papers by Deborah Bird Rose discussed the mythical stories that the Aboriginal communities tell one another about Ned Kelly's 'spiritual significance':

> *No matter how many Captain Cooks, police, and settlers came later, it is unmistakably the case that Ned was here first, actively making the Australian continent ... In spite of the many ambiguities, Ned Kelly – man, myth-dream, and Aboriginal Dreaming figure – provides a superb bridge between cultures.*
>
> (1994: 182)

Edna Griffiths Cargill's book *Glenrowan* makes this concept more porous and topical by repeating a schoolchildren's tale of the Kelly brothers envisioned as Aboriginal peoples from the 'stolen generation' (Cargill 2000: xii). Meanwhile, the Aboriginal artist Freddie Timms (Ngarrmaliny – Janama), in his dot-painting – 'Ned Kelly' (2000) – places Kelly into Aboriginal Dreaming in North-Western Australia; a Nolan-esque square helmet and series of dot circles silhouette the body armour.

As with the Chinese, the later films tend to represent Aboriginal peoples more positively than the novels. In Drewe's novel, which the 2003 Jordan film adapted, Ned likens Aaron Sheritt's suspicious behaviour to that of a black tribesman: 'I've been thinking there's a certain sort of black tribesman I've heard of that reminds me of Aaron' (Drewe 1991: 42). Yet, in Jordan's 2003 film, Ned in voiceover – not included in John Michael McDonagh's published screenplay – recycles this speech to channel his Indigenous ancestors in the preamble to Glenrowan:

> *There's a certain type of black tribesman that bends in the wind ... blends into the background. Mostly he employs the help of the dead ... to destroy other people. The 'Night Dancer', they call him.*

A poignant moment in this film has an outlawed Ned and an Aboriginal Elder pause for a moment as they cross paths in the Wombat Ranges. Ned lowers his revolver; the Elder lowers his weapon. There is no animosity between them; no words of dialogue exchange. Both recognise something familiar in the other: cultural differences aside, each is a symbol of their oppressed community – marginalised by the Crown. After the moment passes, both travel in opposite directions.

Ned in *The Last Outlaw* (1980) declares a similar affection for the Aboriginal peoples. Sitting at a scenic and secluded river with Catherine Lloyd, he explains:

> *The blacks would have known about a place like this, every cave, every spring. With them it's different, it's like they know it before they've ever seen it. A kind of power.*

Cinema-Ned's respect and awe of the Aboriginal peoples certainly corresponds with current attitudes, tolerance and apologies towards Australia's native ancestors; however, beyond the trackers, the Kelly tradition has been unsure about the placement of the Aboriginal peoples into its story. For the most part they are depicted as silent victims of colonisation. Even *Reckless Kelly*'s Aboriginal Uncle Dan (as the exception) is given minimal screen time. The Aboriginal representation in the later films, at most, is symbolic. Yet, such tokenism should not be discredited, for it allows Kelly to be recognised as a spokesmen for 'all' socially oppressed communities – inclusive of the Indigenous, Chinese and Irish selectors. As McQuilton writes, 'if the selectors had feared the gang, or had regarded the outbreak as a criminal outburst, the gang's run would have been brief' (McQuilton 1979: 151). Despite the early films dismissing the Chinese and Aboriginal sympathisers as a minority drawn from criminal classes, the later films represent them as cutting through socio-economic and racial divisions. In these films, the outbreak galvanises Ned's community because it gives rural discontent a focus and broadens it. In such depictions, supporting Ned becomes a defiant rebellion against British hegemony. How cinema-Ned uses his community support to attack this hegemony will be the focus of the final chapter.

Notes

1 For more on the Heidelberg school see *A Treasury of Australian Bush Paintings* (Bruce 1986).

2 For more on these detectives see 'Chinese Detectives' (Presland 1994).

Chapter 6

'Die Like a Kelly, Son': Glenrowan and Trial

Death is not the worst thing that can happen to men.

Plato (Plato: 15)

Ian Jones argues that Glenrowan was the start of a guerrilla campaign and the establishment of a 'Republic'. In the later films, cinema-Ned's idea for Glenrowan comes after some disturbing news about the treatment of his sympathisers: in *The Last Outlaw* (1980) Tom Lloyd explains how nobody named a 'Kelly sympathiser' can purchase land in the North-East. Ned bellows in response: 'they can't do that'. Glenrowan thus becomes his opportunity to instigate a better society; or as McQuilton writes, the first 'pre-political stage in a process that can lead to the development of the insurgent state' (McQuilton 1979: 168). This chapter will discuss how the films represent Glenrowan and the aftermath that led to Kelly's death. While I will continue to discuss Kelly's exhibitionism and showmanship, this chapter will hone in on how the films have reworked many of the historical news sketches from the siege, as a way to promote themselves as historically 'truthful'.

Aaron Sherritt

Glenrowan's preamble included the cold-blooded killing of Aaron Sherritt; it was his punishment for feeding the police vital information about the gang's activities. The sacrifice that all sympathisers must make is to only accept riches from the outlaw himself. To line one's pockets for conspiring with the enemy is the greatest betrayal of all: a true sympathiser should know their place and should prefer death than deceit. In Jordan's 2003 film, Aaron Sherritt is murdered for acting the 'big-shot, instead of a shit-kicker's son like us'. Anchored to the international outlaw tradition, Sherritt is the continuum of the outlaw traitor from past myths. Yet, unlike so many of his traitor cousins that strike the fatal blow to end a bandit's outlawry – Robert Ford in the Jesse James story is the best example – Sherritt neither achieved such fate nor fame.

'His name has a splendid ring of villainy to it and his best-known portrait shows an avaricious, almost cruel face, with sensual lips, cold eyes, and dark hair glossed back from a devilish widow's peak', wrote Jones of Sherritt in *The Fatal Friendship* (I. Jones 1992: vii). Played by Rupert Kathner in *The Glenrowan Affair* (1951) (under the pseudonym 'Hunt Angels') and Harry Southwell in *When the Kellys Were Out* (1923), Sherritt was initially portrayed as a wicked and sneaky conspirator – with no real allegiance to Kelly. By the timing of Jordan's 2003 film, however, Sherritt had become more complicated, more complex and more crucial to the story as a whole. This required more experienced actors (other than Kathner and Southwell) to successfully execute the role: Ken Shorter in Richardson's *Ned Kelly* (1970), Peter Hehir in *The Last Outlaw* (1980) and Joel Edgerton in Jordan's *Ned Kelly* (2003). Demonstrated by this following dialogue from Jordan's 2003 *Ned Kelly*, Sherritt is a confused and broken man who only betrays Ned after his arrest, police bashing and (false) assurances made by Superintendent Hare:

> *I hear you're planning on getting married. Starting a family. Well, I'll tell you lad, your lack of co-operation will make it hard for me to get you out of here and get you back to that girl of yours. And I don't need to tell you about the reward, Aaron. It's a lot of money and I know you could use it. You're a friend of Joe Bryne, aren't you? You've known him since you were children, served time with him. I'm right about that, aren't I? Aaron, it's the Kellys we want. We don't care about Joe. But if it comes right down to it, he'll be shot down like the others. The only chance your friend has depends on you. You can save him if you want to. If you help me with this I'll guarantee his safety.*

Hare makes no such assurances for Sherritt's safety – the bait to lure the gang. The gang, ironically, had similar plans for Sherritt – the bait to lure the police. The murder of Sherritt is simply making the 'obvious choice': 'he has to die', Joe demands in *The Last Outlaw* (1980). Joe further insists to be the one to strike the fatal blow. While Stringybark proves Joe is

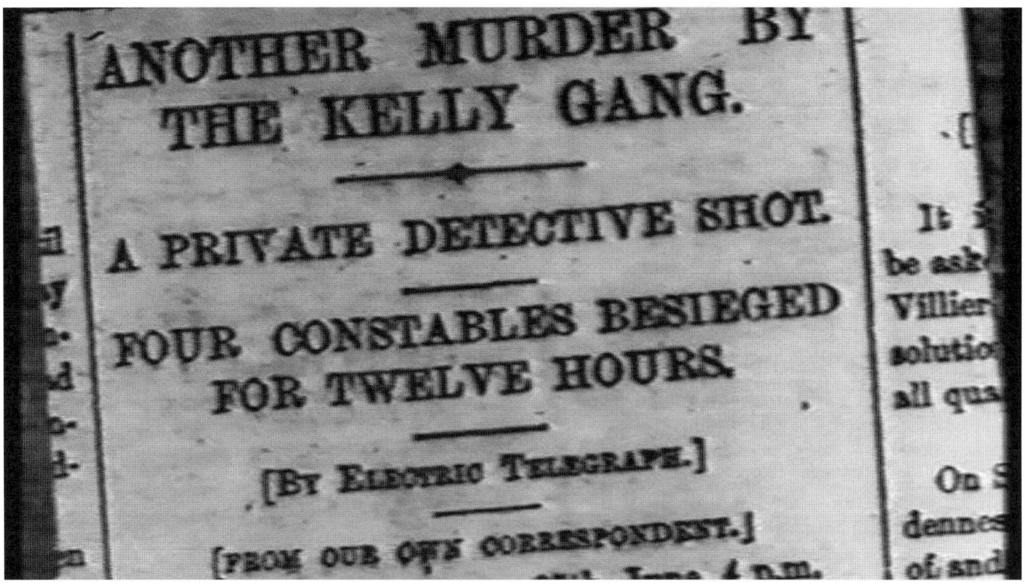
ANOTHER MURDER BY THE KELLY GANG.

A PRIVATE DETECTIVE SHOT.

FOUR CONSTABLES BESIEGED FOR TWELVE HOURS.

[By Electric Telegraph.]

[From our own Correspondent.]

Figure 6.1: News reports (*The Glenrowan Affair*, 1951).

willing to die for Ned, Sherritt's death proves his willingness to kill for him. Nevertheless, no matter how it is reasoned, there is really no excusing Sherritt's death as anything but 'Cold-Blooded Murder'. To sensationalise the scene (and banner Ned as 'Murderer'), *The Glenrowan Affair* (1951) includes a montage of actual newspaper articles from the outbreak; one hysterically inaccurate report even promotes Sherritt to the rank of 'Private Detective'.

A Thomas Carrington news illustration, composed shortly after the shooting – reprinted in Carlyon's promotional book of Jones's miniseries – evidently informs the filmic staging of Sherritt's death (Carlyon 1980: 52). This engraving is accurate, barring one fatal error: Dan's actual position was at the side door of Sherritt's shanty – not the front door. *The Last Outlaw* (1980) corrects this error, despite creating some of its own. Here Joe does not shoot Aaron in the neck, as correctly depicted by Carrington, but the stomach; this certainly stages a more humane murder (if such a thing is possible). The 7-network television station, wary of offending their prime-time audience, would have surely favoured this to the grotesque graphic of Sherritt's neck splattering across the room.

Figure 6.2: Thomas Carrington (1880) 3 July. 'The Murder of Sherritt'. *Illustrated Australian News:* 97.

To ease their guilt, by excusing it as a strategic political move in their grand plan – to launch the North-Eastern Republic – in Jordan's 2003 film, Ned's voice-over explains: 'our plan was to take on Hare and the Victoria police force, the whole bloody lot of them. But to bring them to where we wanted them we needed bait. And the bait was Aaron'. Sherritt's murder is unpleasant, but necessary nonetheless, as is the plan to derail the Special Police Train which is politically excused as guerrilla war, not mass murder. 'It's war, open outright declared war', he rationalises in Richardson's 1970 film.

Preamble

Kelly's Cameron letter concluded with the first suggestion that a railroad attack had been festering. 'Remember your railway', he chillingly insisted; and certainly the films play up this railroad binary by representing the train as a motif identified with law and order. Constable Hare's first appearance in Jordan's 2003 film has him depart his train at Melbourne's Spencer Street Station. Then in another scene (opposite the Special Police Train, again at Spencer Street Station, ready for its outbound journey to Glenrowan) he warns his troopers about the gang's savagery: 'underestimate them and it be you who is "shot down like a dog"', he warns in rebuttal to a cheeky officer's quip, and obviously lamenting the Stringybark police slayings.

At the other end of their journey, Kelly forced his ganger hostages to rip out some train tracks – to ensure that the Special Police Train would derail as it passed through Glenrowan. In a sketch from the *Australian Pictorial Weekly*, Ned points his revolver at the gangers ('My orders must be obeyed', he concluded in the Jerilderie letter) (Figure 6.3). This image

Figure 6.3: (1880) 10 July. 'The Kellys at Glenrowan, Preparing to "Smash the Train"'. *Australian Pictorial Weekly*: 41.

Figure 6.4: (1906). Pulling up the Line at Glenrowan – *The Story of the Kelly Gang*. National Film & Sound Archive: 451069–7.

of the tracks being vandalised has remained a staple of the films: a promotional postcard featuring a still from the 1906 *Story of the Kelly Gang* illustrates the gang, more than just Ned, surrounding the gangers with their revolvers drawn (Figure 6.4) . The necessity to hold the gangers at gun-point is significant, for they are not merely anonymous townsfolk who could be accused of being 'Kelly Sympathisers', but, official railway workers: men working on behalf of and for the Crown. The cruel irony here is that civil-servants are forced to destroy government property, thus killing a train-load of civil-servants in the form of the Victoria Police.

If not for schoolteacher Thomas Curnow (another civil-servant), who warned the train of its hazard just metres ahead, Kelly's bloodthirsty plans would have been realised. Lionising Curnow's 'brave' efforts, *The Story of the Kelly Gang*'s 1906 programme booklet celebrates him as a commendable hero: 'thus taking his life into his hands, he proceeds along the railway and stops the pilot engine and Thank God he saved the Train' (J. Tait and Tait 1906: 2). In gratitude to Curnow's bravery, the Kelly Reward Board renumerated him £550. Only Superintendent Hare, who led the hunt, received a higher amount (£800). In order to heroise Kelly, the later films distort the sentiment of Curnow's noble deed, by reducing the schoolteacher into a sickly little gimp – crippled from an ailing hip deficiency. Telling a fib about his chronically ill wife, and due to Ned feeling 'sorry for the little fella' (as he sighs in Richardson's 1970 film), Curnow is granted permission to leave before the Special Train from Spencer Street arrives. ('Right you can go, but straight home', Ned instructs.) Despite such a gesture causing Joe some unease, as does the armour ('I always said this armour would bring us grief'), its purpose is to amplify Ned's benevolence and goodwill towards others: those he deems to be less fortunate. To not grant Curnow permission to nurse his sick wife would have done little to plaudit Ned as anything but mean-hearted. Yet, allowing Curnow to go ensures that Ned fails because – as Jones argues of history-Kelly – 'he was neither ruthless nor cold-blooded; and in that failure he achieved true greatness' (I. Jones 2002: vii).

Glenrowan

The armoured suits – produced specifically for the Glenrowan gun battle and donned as a necessity after Curnow stopped the train – symbolise the gunfight as a political duel, more than a standard shootout. Part of the mythology behind the suits, is their attachment to other historical global rebellions. In Jordan's 2003 film, the concept is seemingly formed by Ned leafing through images of ancient Chinese warrior armour in a book belonging to the Euroa bank manager Mr Scott. The location of this book – in the gentry's home – allows it to become a symbol of war rather than lawlessness. There is certainly much historical backing to support speculation that Chinese warrior suits inspired the Kelly Gang armour: in 1873, Kelly attended the Prince of Wales Birthday Carnival in Beechworth; there the 3000 locals and 7000 visitors saw an extravagant procession about which *The Beechworth Ovens and Murray Advertiser* marvelled:

> *The Chinese made a show in the procession which has never been equalled ... To use a familiar phrase they took the shine out of all others who took part in the ceremony. The glorious materials and the exquisite handiworks of the exhibits were beyond praise. No European loom, and no European fingers could have produced such results.*
>
> (13 November 1873: 2)

The armour that Ned studies in Jordan's 2003 film is the very same that paraded through Beechworth in 1873. And despite the fact that the armour that he creates is not an exact replica, its design is apparent: it grasps the upper torso and hangs in sections from the waist; an apron piece, slung by straps from the bottom of the breastplate, protects the loins.

Hobsbawm describes Kelly's armour as an eternal image: 'a ghostly figure, tragic, menacing and fragile in his homemade armour, crossing and re-crossing the sun-bleached Australian hinterland, waiting for death' (Hobsbawm 2000: 143). Fetishising the armour even more, Jones fantasises: 'a figure from the dreams of his allies, from the nightmares of his enemies. Myth, legend and reality were fused into a preposterous icon' (I. Jones 1992: 158). For Hobsbawm and Jones, the armour is not a separate and removable artefact in and of itself (even though that it physically is). It rather symbolises Kelly as some kind of colonial Don Quixote; he becomes a duellist of battles, which he could never win, in which his armour could never save him. The armour, which the comedies exaggerate even more, amplifies Kelly to a larger-than-life myth, allowing him to be symbolised with a certain abstraction.

The helmets in the comedies come from ordinary domestic household items: a rubbish bin in *Reckless Kelly* (1993) and a letterbox in *Ned* (2003). As one of its many fetishisations of trash, his body suit in *Reckless Kelly* is appropriately patched from the scrap metal that is scattered around Reckless Island. Fantastically eliminating cinema-Ned's need to shoot his victims, as well as exonerating him from any malicious killing, in both comedies the armour has the extraordinary ability to ricochet bullets onto the shooter. Spotlighting him as the 'star', in *Ned* (2003) no other member wears any protective armour. Jones understands history-Kelly's conceptualisation was to see the armour used for future strike operations: the four armoured outlaws would perform the role of 'storm troopers' (I. Jones 2002: 212). Although history-Kelly never put such quixotic ideas into action, dressed in his armour in *Reckless Kelly* (1993) and *Ned* (2003), cinema-Ned performs a variety of ('storm trooper') bank raids; the comedies' armour is lightweight, mobile and perfect for a bail up and quick getaway. For the historical films, however, that realistically depict the 44-kilogram armour's weight and its burdensome mobility, Ned during his final shootout has no alternative than to stagger like a drunkard as bullets puncture his unprotected arms, legs and groin.

The most engrossing example of the armour is the 1906 *Story of the Kelly Gang*. Cocooned by his amazing iron suit – boasted by the programme booklet as 'the actual armour as worn by Ned Kelly' – the bushranger swaggers from side-to-side towards the camera's position behind a fallen log (Bertrand and Routt 2007: 27). Kelly's forward momentum allows the lens to change perspective: from long shot to mid-shot and then to medium close-up. With a blazing revolver in each hand, the armoured bushranger, dressed in riding boots and a long jacket, approaches a team of police officers, wedged between the camera and a fallen tree. As marvelled by Routt, this image in the history of world cinema became an 'instantly recognisable Australian cinematic icon' (Routt 1999b: 473). Endearingly remembered also as a momentous moment in Australian film history, Kelly's journey to the fallen log compels the (cowardly) police to run out of shot and seemingly behind the camera for protection. They emerge only after he steps over the log and is brought to his knees by a bullet to his leg. This actual log, historically, represents an important artefact in the Kelly 'outbreak' for it marks the exact location of Kelly's 'last stand'. And yet, another instance of misinformation in the film's promotional material was it declaring how the film-makers had used the 'actual' log from the 'outbreak'. In the later films, the robust bushranger during his last stand is reduced into a bullet-ridden mess, in scenes mirroring news sketches from the outbreak. Thomas Carrington's illustration at Glenrowan aptly titled, 'Ned Kelly After the Removal of His Armour', forecasts Kelly's time to death to be imminent (Figure 6.5). A striking feature of Carrington's engraving, and replicated without much modification in *The Last Outlaw* (1980), is Kelly's dandy attire of pinstriped-strapped riding pants, Crimean flannel shirt, waistcoat and high-heeled boots (Figure 6.6). News coverage from the outbreak made similar assertions.

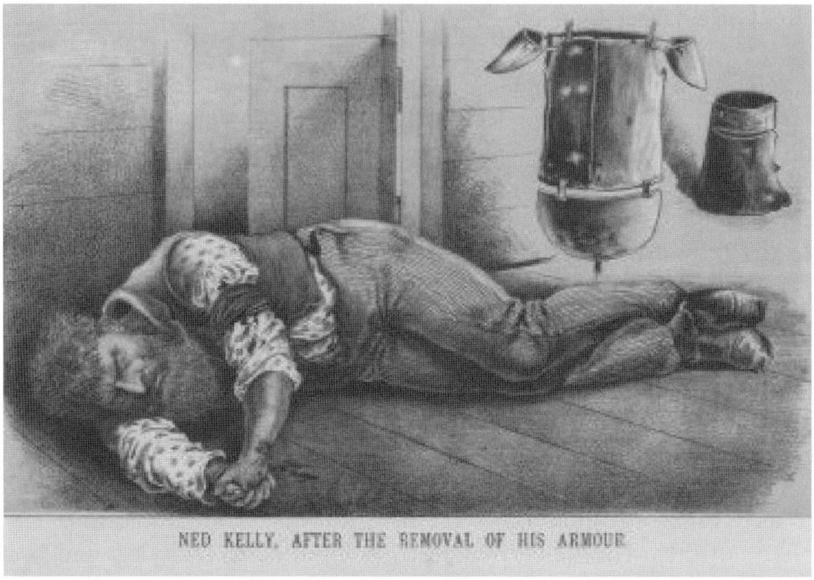

Figure 6.5: Thomas Carrington (1880) 29 June. 'Ned Kelly After the Removal of His Armour'. National Library of Australia. *Canberra: 8420640.*

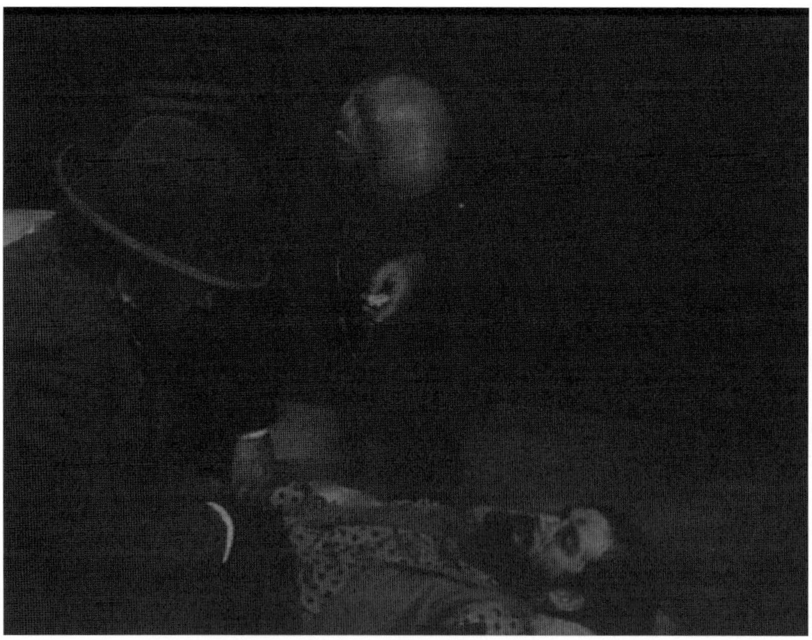

Figure 6.6: Ned lies mortally wounded (*The Last Outlaw*, 1980).

Trial

How outlaws confront death is often their lasting legacy. Joseph Campbell opines:

> *The last act in the biography of the hero is that of death or departure. Here the whole sense of the life is epitomised. Needless to say, the hero would be no hero if death held for him terror; the first consideration is reconciliation with the grave.*
>
> (Campbell 1973: 356)

Regarding Kelly's social bandit myth, the sketcher Julian Ashton's engraving of the criminal trial ('Ned Kelly in the Dock') was quite seminal: he envisioned a well-groomed and politely mannered fellow – the sort of fellow that could easily pass as a lawyer of the defence or a gentleman of intellectual pursuits (Figure 6.7). This illustration seems incomparable to the ravenous and hirsute bushman of Glenrowan. His hair is trimmed short, and although his beard remains long and bushy, it is shaped into the style of a respectable statesman or a politician even. During the outbreak, Thomas Carrington had composed a number of Kelly sketches for the Melbourne *Punch*; often he satirised the unruly bushranger masquerading as a gentleman. In fancy clothes from one sketch, he lectured to the police and became an appropriate replacement for the often-absent Premier (Graham Berry). No such lampooning satire is apparent in Ashton's courtroom sketch, however. One hand attached to the lapel of his jacket (as one would when standing to order) the other clasps the dock's railing. The films which spend some time with the trial all mirror Kelly's stance and general demeanour from Ashton's seminal illustration: *Ned Kelly* (1970), *The Trial of Ned Kelly* (1977) and *The Last Outlaw* (1980).

Figure 6.7: Julian Ashton (1880) 28 August. 'Ned Kelly in the Dock'. *Illustrated Australian News*: 145.

By restaging this illustration, however, the films are able to take it further by giving cinema-Ned motion and speech. In Richardson's 1970 film, Jagger recites a variety of cheeky one-liners, which history-Kelly did actually speak during the trial. ('I fear death as little as to drink a cup of tea'; 'my mind is as easy and clear as it possibly can be'.) This dialogue becomes significant in such scenes, more significant than other scenes, because here one can listen to words, lines and paragraphs that were actually spoken, at one point, by history-Kelly. Such a scene, therefore, does not just become a staging of the trial, but a re-enactment of it with the actual dialogue used as a guide. Furthermore, the dialogue is used as 'categorical' evidence that Kelly did face his death with good grace. To enhance this point further, Richardson concludes his 1970 film with a freeze frame of Jagger grinning into the camera in response to Justice Barry announcing the sentence of death. 'I'll see you there', he coolly retorts. The end.

The film that really explores the court proceedings is the telefilm *The Trial of Ned Kelly* (1977). Since there was no official transcript taken of the trial, Roger Simpson's teleplay was adapted from the longhand 'Notes of the Evidence' taken by the Judge's Associate, as well as various other Court documents, and newspaper reports from the time. Indicated by the opening shot of the camera panning over the police corpses at Stringybark creek, Ned is on trial for his involvement in these three deaths. From here, the film cuts to a manacled Ned, incarcerated and no longer a roaming bushranger. Moments later, the procession towards the gallows culminates with him sighing 'oh well … I s'ppose it has come to this'. And here the telefilm's rhetorical question (rhetorical because the answer is overstated and apparent) is introduced: was Kelly just the victim of his own misfortune – or the victim of a corrupt and compromised criminal trial? From this scene, the film returns, now in flashback, to the beginning of the trial. ('All stand' hollers the crier in voice-over.)

This telefilm is more accurately a docudrama. Its narrator – played by Alan Hopgood, who speaks in his Australian brogue – mostly fills in back story and narrative exposition. Pausing the trial, he explains the injustice of the proceedings and that Kelly was 'a legend in his own time'. As a constant reminder of its didactic docudrama genre, the actors do not just acknowledge the narrator (dressed in modern clothes) but become frustrated by his insistent interruptions; they are forced to silently wait until he is ready for them to recommence. In this telefilm, the trial becomes less about Kelly and more about his opposers. Witnesses deposing their evidence dominate the scenes; a silent (yet highly visible) Ned scoffs in the background. *The Last Outlaw* (1980) and Richardson's 1970 film, as a point of difference, are only interested in Kelly's theatrics and banter with Justice Barry. And while this banter does appear in the *Trial of Ned Kelly* (1977), it is hurried along more than celebrated as the trial's great moment. Barry, furthermore, is foregrounded as the film's villain; he never even gives the jury an opportunity to consider the option of 'self-defence'. ('Your verdict must be either guilty of murder or acquittal'.) So with that, the narrator explains how they reached the 'inevitable verdict of guilty' before too long. As a final scene, the narrator is transported to 1977; standing in a contemporary, and empty courtroom, he sardonically explains Barry's demise. ('After what was explained as a short and unexpected illness, he died to face his judgement by a "higher court"'.)

The argument made by this telefilm is that had Kelly received a more experienced barrister than Henry Bindon – pulled up often by the narrator for his failure to expose the flaws of the prosecution – or not appointed Justice Barry who had sentenced Mrs Kelly to three-years-hard-labour over the Fitzpatrick incident, then perhaps the jury would have reached a different verdict. Perhaps. Adding weight to this argument is John Castles's posthumously released history book, *Ned Kelly's Last Days* (Castles 2005). This publication is quite engrossing, not just for its ability to unpack the corruption that punctuated the trial, but its refusal to lionise Kelly as some great unsung hero. The bushranger, he argues, is someone who deserved punishment – but not an unfair trial. Castles opines that the trial's kangaroo court provides history-Kelly unnecessary sympathy simply because he was not shown the courtesy any citizen of a democratic judicial system should expect.

The trial raises a case for Kelly's unfair persecution, which is why it hardly appears in any of the early films. *The Kelly Gang* (1919) is the only early film to include the trial, albeit for a fleeting moment. Included as a coda, the only extract shown is Justice Barry (played by Harry Southwell who also doubles as Aaron Sherritt) mouthing his sentence, 'death by hanging'. There is no illustration of a verbal exchange between the accused and judge, and no evidence that the trial was handled unethically. The difference here is Ned's own admission of guilt, and remorse. The scene before this concludes at Glenrowan with the bushranger conceding to the righteous-hand of law and order.

Death

No longer willing to live on the margin of the margins, cinema-Ned in the early films accepts that his 'kind' must be exterminated or reformed – if the morally weak can even be saved. There is nothing in any of these early films to demonstrate the contrary. Ned concedes that father-knows-best, and consents to the punishment. In doing so, he becomes no more extraordinary than any other bushranger that succumbed to a similar fate. In 1919, capital punishment was so accepted that the callousness of the hanging in Southwell's film is never questioned or lamented. A long-shot showing the noose placed around Ned's neck hardly encourages any pathos – or represents his death as anything more tragic than the other 104 executions staged on the gallows at the Melbourne Gaol. Rhetorical indeed, but one question that such an image encourages to ask: is the life of outlawry at all glamorous? This sentiment certainly echoes Rolf Boldrewood's seminal novel *Robbery Under Arms* (Boldrewood 1882), whose plot follows the ventures of the foolhardy Marston brothers, Jim and Dick. Seduced into a life of bushranging, by the alluring career criminal Captain Starlight, they come to regret their felonious ways. Too late for Jim – shot dead along with Starlight in a shootout – Dick, expected to hang, is given a reduced sentence of 15 years and released, literally, into the arms of his fiancé Gracy Storefield. The difference from the early

Kelly films, however, is that Ned was a career criminal in the tradition of Starlight. Death for such a character is the only option; but, only after he accepts guilt and seeks redemption, which, paradoxically, he is never granted. Only death. The later films, in contrast, are more tragic because Ned has done nothing wrong (in the eyes of his community) and he has nothing to redeem.

Ned Kelly (1970), *The Trial of Ned Kelly* (1977) and *The Last Outlaw* (1980) include Kelly's death as a means to film the earlier out-of-bounds interior of the Melbourne Gaol. Until 1929, the gaol was an active prison, and was reopened during World War II to house offending servicemen (Riddett and Down 1991: 29). Becoming the property of the National Trust in 1957, and opened as a museum in 1972 (Goad 1998: 37), Richardson's footage – shot in 1969 – was the first moving pictures ever taken of its interior. Surely, this goes someway to explain his depiction of the architecture as something greater than just a gothic backdrop to stage the felon's final hours. Foregrounded as the centrepiece, it becomes the milieu for Mrs Kelly to deliver the famous line: 'die like a Kelly, son'. Shot in extreme-long-shot she is diminished by the mammoth construction. Richardson's effect here is quite accurate, for the final conversation between mother and son did not grant any privacy on account of it taking place through the iron grille of Kelly's cell door (Castles 2005: 213). Mrs (Ellen) Kelly's autobiography claims that she was not allowed to touch or kiss her son. Jones understands their goodbye as 'starchy and impersonal' (Balcarek 1984: 105; I. Jones 2002: 283). As point of difference, in *The Last Outlaw* (1980), Ned's final moments with his mother are tender and intimate; in close-up and past his cell door, they stand wrapped in one another's arms. Tears stream from them both as Mrs Kelly instructs: 'die as bravely as you lived', and of course, 'die like a Kelly, son'. To her, he remains a decent and admirable citizen, worthy of sorrow and lament.

Kelly's execution would become the final spectacle of the outbreak. With the gallows marking his stage, a contingent of journalists gathered to report on the dramatic spectacle. Recreating this moment, in *The Last Outlaw* (1980) the journalists eagerly await his final words of remorse and regret, only to behold his defiance as he boldly announces: 'Ah well I suppose it has come to this ... such is life'. The eyewitnesses from the hanging, however, reported on a less than brave Kelly. The Melbourne *Argus* stated – 'It was his intention to make a speech, but his courage evidently failed him, and he merely said, "Ah, well, I suppose it has come to this", as the rope was being placed around his neck' (12 November 1880: 6). The only 'known' historical sketch (but there were probably others) depicting the hanging was Carrington's 'Last Scene of the Kelly Drama' – published on the front cover of *The Australasian Sketcher* on 20 November 1880.

Despite not attending, Carrington completed the engraving from a rough outline by the news journalist Joe Melvin. Jones plaudits this engraving as 'accurate in almost every detail' (I. Jones and Carrington 2003: 30). It certainly informs his 1980 telemovie as well as the *Trial of Ned Kelly* (1977) and Richardson's *Ned Kelly* (1970); none of the filmic representations make any significant amendment (from the original engraving) to the characters' position on the scaffold.

Figure 6.8: Ned arrives on the gallows (*The Last Outlaw*, 1980).

Figure 6.9: Thomas Carrington (1880) 20 November. 'Last Scene of the Kelly Drama: The Criminal on the Scaffold'. *The Australasian Sketcher*: Front Cover.

The first segment of the death in *The Trial of Ned Kelly* (1977) concludes with Ned standing on the gallows. ('Ah well I suppose it has come to this'.) From here the trial, then back again, not to this moment, but, the moment that has just passed. Kelly, now masked by his white cap stands readied for death. Seemingly mournful of Ned's unfortunate trouble, the Governor waits just a bit longer to make all present aware, most of all the condemned felon, of his sympathy. Giving his official nod to the hangman, the lever is pulled, the trap door opens and the rope jerks taut. Narrating the story of a judicial system, which muffled Kelly's own claims and accusations, in this film cinema-Ned – rather than history-Kelly – is given full-voice. Too late for Ned to be saved, the audience is reminded as to why he deserves their sympathy. For this reason, the audience becomes more than passive observers to history on the screen – they are active participants of his enduring legacy. They are modern day Kelly sympathisers.

The death in Richardson's 1970 film occurs at the very beginning and is not returned to in any form. On the gallows, a calm yet sombre Ned allows his legs to be strapped and noose placed around his neck. The only dialogue is the famous Kelly idiom ('such is life'). The hangman pulls the hood over Ned's face; Richardson cuts to a long shot as the body drops from the gallows and into death. The (now) carcass swings for a moment. The film illuminates in full colour to a pre-outlawed Ned gleefully travelling across the bucolic fields. On the screen in white bold letters reads: 'THE BEGINNING'.

Undead

The Last Outlaw (1980) ends its narrative at the hanging; yet, further than *The Trial of Ned Kelly* (1977) lamenting the wrong against Kelly (opposed to Kelly's wrong), this mini-series wants to present some categorical proof that Kelly did make a social and political change. From his death, a tracking shot from the gallows travels down a corridor of inmates caged in their cells, hollering at this spectacle of injustice. Outside the gaol, the small gathering (apparelled in mourning wear) laments the passing of 10am as the moment of his death. Inside the gaol, the carcass, now in an enclosed coffin, is carted across the echoing cobblestones. In voice-over, Ned posthumously reads a passage from a published interview, which he supposedly conducted with his lawyer, David Gaunson, when in gaol:

> *If my life teaches the public that men are made mad by bad treatment, and if the police are taught that they may not exasperate to madness the men they persecute and ill-treat, my life will not be entirely thrown away.*

Following this is an intertitle 'proving' his political and social influence:

> *Four months later, a Royal Commission investigated the Police Force of Victoria and its role in the Kelly Outbreak. The reforms which followed created a tradition of public accountability and self-examination, which endures today.*

So Kelly did change the social landscape, as far as policing was concerned. This is true, however such accountabilities were already in place; they were just not being marshalled. Rather than blame the police, entirely, for their negligence, the Commission's purpose was to ensure another outbreak, of any magnitude, did not cultivate elsewhere. The very purpose of the Commission, nevertheless, does demonstrate the sort of posthumous threat that Kelly posed to the police administration.

To celebrate the fact that Kelly never really died – not in a cultural form anyway – the comedies have the bushranger avoid his death completely. In *Ned* (2003), to supplement his incompetence as a bushman, he utilises his talent as 'the world's premiere outlaw illusionist' to escape his prison cell and live to tell his story. In *Reckless Kelly* (1993), a falling petrol pump crushes his archenemy, Sir John, into the ground and towards the same hell Justice Barry most probably found himself. *Reckless Kelly* (1993), like *The Last Outlaw* (1980), ends with an intertitle celebrating Kelly's enduring legacy. Superimposed onto a moving picture of the Australian coast, it reads: 'This film is dedicated to the irreverent spirit of a great Australian outlaw who championed the rights of the individual against the oppression of authority'.

How Ned Kelly can posthumously survive is a question investigated in all of the films. Perhaps he cannot. In the early films, death is punishment for living a 'dog's life'. By accepting his wrong he accepts the consequence which is death; but, more than accepting that his own behaviour is wrong – death becomes a by-product of outlawry – Ned accepts his core values to be wrong. In the recent historical films, however, Ned's death is not a consequence of his own wrong – but the wrong of a political system that would execute a persecuted man for merely fighting for the rights of his community.

In such films, he does not deserve to die, because, unlike his former screen personae, he has done nothing wrong. To echo Routt, his choices are just the 'obvious choices' – even ambushing and killing three police officers. Yet more than this, he is cultured and intelligent. (His favourite book is *Lorna Doone*.) No longer spending his time in debauchery, he transcends into a valuable member of his community. The later films all include examples of Ned, before his outbreak, as a hardworking manual labourer. As a point of contrast, in the early films, he is never anything but a professional ill-mannered bushranger. Moreover, no matter which manifestation is being discussed, Ned is always a figure bellowing 'no' when everyone is nodding 'yes'. This is his legacy of historical significance – and the reason for why a film like *Reckless Kelly* (1993) would plaudit his 'irreverent spirit'. This also, as Hobsbawm asserts, is why bandits never really die (in a mythical sense):

> *To some extent it expresses the wish that the people's champion cannot be defeated, the same sort of wish that produces the perennial myths of the good king – and the good bandit – who has not really died, but will come back one day to restore justice. Refusal to believe in a robber's death is a certain criterion of his nobility.*
>
> (Hobsbawm 2000: 57)

Cinema-Ned's survival in the comedies illustrates this point: he survives to narrate his own story – albeit as a senile old-coot in Forsythe's 2003 comedy. In the other later films, cinema-Ned does not need to physically survive for his words allow him to remain in nature: 'If my life teaches the public', he exclaims posthumously in *The Last Outlaw* (1980).

Conclusion

What kind of history are the Kelly films? Entertainment history? Cultural history? Cinema history? Rarely are they discussed as serious history – history that seriously penetrates the social consciousness – and never history to equal the importance of written history. A story that seems so cinematic, so filmable, critics are often angered as to why there is yet to be a really great Kelly film; William Routt concludes his review of Jordan's 2003 film wanting 'another Ned Kelly film, one they haven't made yet' (Routt 2003c: 17). But maybe this is the point of Kelly cinema, a point that Ina Bertrand recognised when discussing this same film: 'A *definitive* Kelly film is probably not possible' (Bertrand 2003). The elastic parameters of Kelly's myth are so vast, so wide, how does one even begin to deal with this myth? How does one narrativise it into moving pictures?

The most appropriate comparison to the Kelly myth is not Wyatt Earp (he was a lawman), nor fellow outlaws (Jesse James, Billy the Kid), nor Robin Hood (his myth is purely fiction), but, Elvis Presley. The kaleidoscope of Presley's myth is so luminescent that he becomes too translucent to observe in his entirety. As with Kelly, all the films on Presley have been disappointments; even the 1979 two-part telefilm *Elvis* (Carpenter 1979), starring Kurt Russell in his breakout performance. Glossing over his more questionable behaviour – domestic violence, drug abuse, affairs and curious meetings with President Nixon – this is a continuum of Elvis-the-clean-cut-boy-scout-film-star from his decade as cinema-Elvis. The best film on Presley is Jim Jarmusch's *Mystery Train* (Jarmusch 1989). Not interested in Presley's own rags-to-riches story, set in the period of its production, its vignettes feature a motley crew of vacuous characters that desperately latch onto his myth in search of some greater meaning in their own lives. This film is really about Jarmusch's own negative perception of the Presley commodity: 'Elvis was just a guy and he got elevated to the status of almost a saint, like a Pope or something, because people can make money off that', he said (Marcus 1991: 196).

Abe Forsythe's attitude to Ned Kelly was not entirely dissimilar. Opening his film at a contemporary Glenrowan, he wanted to explore how Kelly has been commodified as something great when he was just 'a guy'; and for Forsythe, a rather immature and vulgar 'guy' to boot. Forsythe's failure, however, was his ineptness to produce something quite as rich as *Mystery Train*. Yet, more than this, Forsythe's great misdirection was transporting his narrative to the period of the outbreak – his critique on Kelly's 'contemporary commodification' to bookend the film is far more interesting.

The problem that every Kelly film has tackled, and the reason for why they are so culturally fascinating, is how they unpack a selection of Kelly histories and media to create an entirely new cultural canvas. Every film taps into the conversation, brouhaha and debate that have been raging since those three policemen were shot dead at Stringybark Creek. Each film provokes broader Kelly dialogues, which are flushed through other forms of the media: talkback radio, newspapers, journal articles and books. No matter what the film is, or how atrocious, or just plain offensive (in a historically inaccurate way), each moots those deeply rooted Kelly questions: Why is he significant? Was he a hero? Why do we still care? Why do films keep appearing? To answer the final question, anyway, the public is not ready to forget Kelly; they remain engaged enough to contribute to the conversations that such questions raise. Through the films, Kelly is effervesced to become many things: an immature twerp (*Ned*, 2003), motorcycle bank robber (*Reckless Kelly*, 1993), pop star (*Ned Kelly*, 1970), grub (*The Kelly Gang*, 1919), footy hero (*The Glenrowan Affair*, 1951), heartthrob (*Ned Kelly*, 2003).

To watch one Kelly film is to watch the history of the cinema, history of the tradition and just history of Ned Kelly. Each is a mediation of the other (and meditation on the other), which is why none are very good. How can something be great when its forefathers are so mediocre, so disappointing. Brian McFarlane would take exception here, for he claims that the films have just failed where literary works have succeeded (McFarlane 2006: 27). (Peter Carey's *The True History of the Kelly Gang* (2000) is the exhausted example, but even that is a somewhat hysterical, bombastic and pretentious reworking of Kelly's Jerilderie letter.) The problem of the films is how the makers (film-makers) become lost in the myth. Affirming this point, Gregor Jordan – at the announcement of his Kelly film – spoke of his 'cultural responsibility' to 'get it right'. Huh? How can greatness come from someone pandering to 'get it right'?

The films are more of a rite than attempts to rip the tradition from its roots and reposition it in a way that will produce an entirely different vantage point, an entirely different conversation. The fascination, nevertheless, of the films is how they sit trapped in that vacuum of Kelly history. Unable to shift, or breathe, or flower, independently they are forever stemmed by his aura. Conscious of this, they make sense of their own purpose by restaging the historical artefacts: the news reports, illustrations, letters and armour. They are difficult (almost impossible) to situate within pre-existing genres and cycles of Australian cinema and world cinema. An entity and sporadic genre in and of themselves, despite attracting some external comparison, they seldom behave in the manner expected of other bushranger films or westerns or even social bandit films. (Only the films since the 1960s are symptomatic of the social bandit locus.) Parables of Kelly as a subject of popular history, they gather awkwardly, and uncomfortably, within their various histories: film history, cultural history and Kelly history.

Part of the problem here is how they are rarely discussed as cinema; more often, they are just inserted into television news stories to fill some blank screen concerning the 'latest historical Kelly finding'. Television viewers seem less familiar with the films as 'cinema'. To encourage filmgoers to watch the films – in their entirety (when possible) – is a difficult task, whence the central endeavour of this book was conceived: to not just marshal the films into the lot of Kelly history, but posit them to be just as important as written Kelly histories. In many regards, the films are incomplete as is all written history; history is only ever a snapshot of its time in history. Mick Jagger's casting may have been a calamitous misfire, but it does present an intriguing portrait of the bushranger: sexy, charismatic, lithe and famous.

With cinema-Ned, one is given the experience of watching the idea of the historical Kelly move and behave. This provides a kind of historical insight and understanding. The purpose of this book has not been to make a claim for the great-unsung Kelly treasure, or celebrate the films' badness. Its purpose has been to unpack how they confront Kelly, and in doing so posit them as telling endeavours of the Kelly myth. To remove them from conversations on Kelly is to remove half the story as to how Ned Kelly is remembered, fetishised and historicised. And to dismiss them as bad cinema is to miss a great opportunity to survey the importance of history films and challenges that such a form presents. The critical problem here is that Kelly cinema cannot be cultivated as one would written history, for its very motion and movement demands an entirely different set of reading practices; its medium is performative rather than descriptive. Words can only ever describe, never can they show. And to change the medium is to change the message: written history can never do what a moving picture can. What happens when the cinema deconstructs and reconstructs history? How is history-Kelly distorted by the experience of watching a walking-talking cinema-Ned?

Perhaps the message of these films (to some degree) is, maybe, just a cautionary tale: history can only ever play with the facts and build meta-narratives between such facts. History is never purely interested in telling the story straight. Every historian has a claim to make – a point to prove. Every historian has a story to tell. Written history does not hold the copyright to history; it is open and available to anyone and everyone. And woven into such an approach is the very idea that no particular type or medium of history is any greater than its 'other'. Nor is it more worthy of analysis. The very notion as to why Kelly films remain a staple of the Australian cinema – and the Kelly tradition for that matter – is what they are able to do with the Kelly legend. Not 'print the legend', to echo *The Man Who Shot Liberty Valance* (Ford 1962), but, 'show the legend' as a living, breathing, moving and dying artefact of popular history.

Appendix: Cast and Crew

‘The Perth Fragment’

Production Year	1906

****

The Story of the Kelly Gang

Production Year	1906
Premiere	26 December, 1906, Melbourne
Director	Charles Tait
Producer	J and N Tait/Johnson and Gibson
Screenwriter	Charles Tait

Cast

Ned Kelly	Frank Mills/Canadian Stunt Actor
Dan Kelly	Sam Crew
John Forde	Mr Marshall
Steve Hart	Jack Ennis
Mr McKenzie	Norman Campbell
Joe Byrne	Will Coyne
Aaron Sherritt	Norman Campbell
Kate Kelly	Lizzie Tait
Head of Police	Charles Tait
Sergeant	John Forde
Detective	L A O Haslett
Policeman	Norman Campbell
Banker	Mr Veitch
Sandy Gloster	Norman Campbell

****

The Story of the Kelly Gang

Production Year	1910
Director	William Gibson and Millard Johnson
Producer	Johnson and Gibson
Screenwriter	Johnson and Gibson

Cast

Ned Kelly	Frank Mills
Dan Kelly	Mr Marshall
Steve Hart	Mr McKenzie, Jack Ennis
Joe Byrne	Will Coyne
Aaron Sherritt	Norman Campbell
Policeman	Norman Campbell
Sandy Gloster	Norman Campbell

****

The Kelly Gang

Production Year	1919
Premiere	21 February, 1920, Sydney
Director	Harry Southwell
Producer	Harry Southwell
Screenwriter	Harry Southwell
Production Company	Southwell Screen Plays

Cast

Ned Kelly	Godfrey Cass
Dan Kelly	Upton Brown
Joe Byrne	Horace Crawford
Sergeant Kennedy	Thomas Sinclair
Kate Kelly	Adele Inman
Constable McIntyre	Cyril Inman
Aaron Sherritt	Robert Inman
Mrs Kelly	Maud Appleton
Sergeant Steele	Harry Southwell

****

When the Kellys Were Out

Production Year	1923
Premiere	9 July, 1923, Adelaide
Director	Harry Southwell
Producer	Harry Southwell
Screenwriter	Harry Southwell
Production Company	Australian Players Film Co.

Cast

Ned Kelly	Godfrey Cass
Kate Kelly	Rose Rooney
Aaron Sherritt	Harry Southwell
Dan Kelly	Charles Villiers
Steve Hart	William Ellison
Joe Byrne	Allan Douglas
Constable McIntyre	Fred Twitcham
Sergeant Steel	Syd Everett
Sergeant Kennedy	Mervyn Barrington
Fitzpatrick	W Ryan
Judge Redmond Barry	David Edelsten

****

When the Kellys Rode

Production Year	1934
Premiere	23 June, 1934, Brisbane
Director	Harry Southwell
Producer	Harry Southwell
Screenwriter	Harry Southwell
Production Company	Imperial Feature Films

Cast

Ned Kelly	Hay Simpson
Dan Kelly	John Appleton

Joe Byrne	Norman Wait
Steve Hart	Robert Inglis
Sergeant Steele	George Randall
Kate Kelly	Regina Somerville
Blacksmith	Stan Tolhurst

****

The Glenrowan Affair

Production Year	1951
Premiere	17 August, 1951, Sydney
Director	Rupert Kathner
Producer	Rupert Kathner
Screenwriter	Rupert Kathner
Production Company	Australian Action Pictures

Cast

Ned Kelly	Bob Chitty
Joe Byrne	Albie Henderson
Dan Kelly	Ben Crowe
Steve Hart	Bill Wright
Aaron Sherritt	Rupert Kathner
Father Gibney	John Fernside
Commissioner Nicholson	Charles Tasman
Superintendent Hare	Charles Webb
Superintendent Standish	Edward Smith
Sergeant Steele	Frank Ransome
Blacksmith	Stan Tolhurst
Kate Kelly	Beatrice Kay
Mrs Skillion	Wendy Roberts
Aaron Sherritt	Hunt Angels (Rupert Kathner)
Mrs Anne Jones	Dora Norris
Narrator	Charles Tingwell

****

Ned Kelly

Production Year	1970
Premiere	28 July 1970, Glenrowan
Director	Tony Richardson
Producer	Neil Hartley
Screenwriter	Tony Richardson and Ian Jones
Production Company	Woodfall Film Productions

Cast

Ned Kelly	Mick Jagger
Mrs Kelly	Clarissa Kaye-Mason
Joe Byrne	Mark McManus
Supt Nicholson	Ken Goodlet
Judge Barry	Frank Thring
George King	Bruce Barry
Mr Scott	Tony Bazell
Dan Kelly	Allen Bickford
Sergeant Steele	Robert Bruning
McInnes	Alexander Cann
Curnow	David Copping
Maggie Kelly	Diane Craig
Father O'Hea	Gerry Duggan
Steve Hart	Geoff Gilmour
Mrs Devine	Anne Harvey

****

The Last Outlaw

Production Year	1980
Premiere	15 October, 1980
Director	Kevin James Dobson and George Miller
Producer	Ian Jones and Bronwyn Binns
Screenwriter	Ian Jones and Bronwyn Binns
Production Company	Pegasus Productions

Cast

Ned Kelly	John Jarratt
Joe Byrne	Steve Bisley
Mrs Kelly	Elaine Cusick
Dan Kelly	John Ley
Steve Hart	Ric Herbert
Aaron Sherritt	Peter Hehir
Maggie Kelly	Debra Lawrance
Kate Kelly	Sigrid Thornton
Tom Lloyd	Lewis Fitz-Gerald
Sergeant Steele	Tim Elliott
George King	Paul Mason
Harry Power	Gerard Kennedy
Annie	Jacki Kerin
Jim	Paul Trahair
Grace	Kaarin Fairfax

****

Reckless Kelly

Production Year	1993
Premiere	8 April, 1993, Sydney
Director	Yahoo Serious
Producer	Warwick Ross
Screenwriter	Lulu Pinkus, David Roach, Warwick Ross and Yahoo Serious
Production Company	Serious Entertainment Pty Ltd

Cast

Ned Kelly	Yahoo Serious
Robin Banks	Melora Hardin
Major Wib	Alexei Sayle
Sir John	Hugo Weaving
Mrs Delance	Kathleen Freeman
Sam Delance	John Pinette
Dan Kelly	Bob Maza

Ernie the Fan	Martin Ferrero
Joe Kelly	Anthony Ackroyd
Miss Twisty	Tracy Mann

****

Ned Kelly

Production Year	2002/3
Premiere	27 March, 2003, Melbourne
Director	Gregor Jordan
Producer	Nelson Woss and Lynda House
Screenwriter	John Michael McDonagh
Production Company	Working Title Films

Cast

Ned Kelly	Heath Ledger
Joseph Byrne	Orlando Bloom
Superintendent Francis Hare	Geoffrey Rush
Julia Cook	Naomi Watts
Aaron Sherritt	Joel Edgerton
Dan Kelly	Laurence Kinlan
Steve Hart	Philip Barantini
Kate Kelly	Kerry Condon
Ellen Kelly	Kris McQuade
Grace Kelly	Emily Browning
Constable Fitzpatrick	Kiri Paramore
Susan Scott	Rachel Griffiths
Robert Scott	Geoff Morrell
Premier Graham Berry	Charles 'Bud' Tingwell
Jane Jones	Saskia Burmeister

****

Ned

Production Year	2003
Premiere	23 May, 2003, Sydney

Director	Abe Forsythe
Producer	Darryl Robinson
Screenwriter	Abe Forsythe
Production Company	Ocean Pictures Pty Limited

Cast

Ned Kelly	Abe Forsythe
Sinclair	Felix Williamson
Steve Hart/Orderly	Damon Herriman
Dan Kelly/Tour Bus Guide	Nick Flint
Joe Byrne/Orderly	Josef Ber
Mr Kelly	Jeremy Sims
Mrs Kelly	Caitlin McDougall
Narrator	Drew Forsythe
Muffy	Michala Banas
Tim Richards	Hawkins/Ned Kelly World Ned
Young Boy	Shaun Loseby
Henchman Shanahan	Ryan Johnson
Henchman Williams	Michael Falzon
Henchman Byrne	Sean Lynch
Henchman Morrissey	Septimus Caton

Works Cited

(1873). *The Beechworth Ovens and Murray Advertiser* (13 November): 2.
(1874). *The Beechworth Ovens and Murray Advertiser* (13 November): 1.
(1878). 'Finding of Sergeant Kennedy's Body'. *The Argus* (1 November): 6.
(1878). *The Argus* (4 November): 6.
(1878). 'The Police Murders'. *The Argus* (11 November): 7.
(1878). 'The Police Murders'. *The Argus* (13 November): 6.
(1878). 'Two Constables Shot Dead and Missing'. *The Argus* (23 October): 5.
(1878). 'The Atrocious Murders of Police'. *The Argus* (27 December): 3.
(1878). 'Atrocious Murders by Bushrangers'. *The Argus* (29 October): 5.
(1879). 'About the Kellys'. *Beechworth Newspaper* (11 January): 8.
(1879). *Brisbane Courier* (28 August): 28.
(1879). *The Argus* (29 March): 3.
(1880). *The Bulletin* (3 July): 9.
(1880). 'Edward Kelly Before the Police Court'. *The Argus* (10 August): 7.
(1880). 'The Condemned Bushranger'. *The Argus* (10 November): 6.
(1880). 'The Execution of Edward Kelly'. *The Argus* (12 November): 6.
(1880). *The Australasian Sketcher* (17 July): 167.
(1880). 'The Trial of Edward Kelly'. *The Argus* (20 September): 7.
(1880). 'The Kelly Gang'. *The Argus* (22 May): 5.
(1880). 'Another Kelly Outrage: Cold-Blooded Murder'. *The Argus* (28 June): 5.
(1906). 'The Kelly Gang'. *The Argus* (27 December): 5.
(1907). 'News of the Day'. *The Bulletin* (24 January): 8.
(1928). Report of the Royal Commission on the Moving Picture Industry in Australia. Canberra: Government of Commonwealth of Australia.
(1934). 'Belated Hush Hush about Our Bushrangers'. *The Australian Women's Weekly* (19 May): 2.
(1934). 'Review'. *The Brisbane Telegraph* (22 June): 5.
(1948). 'When the Kellys Rode'. *Film Weekly* (8 July): 23.
(1951). 'The Glenrowan Affair'. *Sunday Herald* (9 August): 5.
(1968). Police Commission: Minutes of Evidence Taken Before Royal Commission on the Police Force of Victoria. Melbourne: Heinemann.
(1993). *Reckless Kelly Original Motion Picture Soundtrack*. Australia: (Sound Recording). Universal.
(2003). *Ned Original Motion Picture Soundtrack*. Australia: (Sound Recording). Sony.
Adams, Francis (1968), 'The Labour Movement in Australia', in *The Australian Dream*, edited by I. Turner. Melbourne: Sun Books.
Allen, Vince, and Carolyn Allen (2002), *Burnt to a Cinder, was I*, Melbourne: Artisans Attic.

Amenta, Pino (1976), *The Sullivans*, Australia: Crawford Productions.

Anderson, Lindsay (1963). *This Sporting Life*. Britain: Julian Wintle/Leslie Parkyn Productions.

Ashmead, Joseph (1922), *The Briars and Thorns: The True Story of the Kelly Gang*, Melbourne: ms. PA BOX 55 with PA 02/28, State Library of Victoria.

Baker, W. T. (1920), 'The Kelly Gang', *The Theatre Magazine*, 28 March.

Balcarek, Dagmar (1984), In *Ellen Kelly: A Biography in Novel Form as seen from a Woman's and Mother's Point of View*, edited by M. Brunato and N. Green. Glenrowan: Farlell.

Bamblett, Colin (1971), 'The Social Bandit in the Bushranging History of NSW and Victoria 1860–1880' (MA), University of Western Australia, Perth.

Barber, Lynden (1999). '"Sociopath" Kelly to Get Big-Screen Justice at Last'. *The Australian* (10 April): 3.

——— (2003), 'Kelly Culture – Why the Legend Grows – Behind the Mask'. *The Australian* (1 March): 5.

Barber, Noel (1964), 'Sidney Nolan', in *Conversations with Painters*. London: Collins: 83–100.

Bateman, Mary (1980), 'The Lincoln-Cass Films', *Cinema Papers*, June–July: 170–175.

Bayonas, Lynn (1969–1976), *Division 4*. Australia: Crawford Productions.

Belden, H. M. (ed.) (1940), *Ballads and Songs Collected by the Missouri Folklore Society*, Columbia: University of Missouri.

Benedek, Laslo (1953), *The Wild One*, America: Stanley Kramer Productions.

Bennetts, Don (1970), *Ned Kelly: The Making of the Myth*, Australia: ABC.

Bertrand, Ina (1978), *Film Censorship in Australia*, Queensland: University of Queensland Press.

——— (1980), 'The Essential Cinematic Ned', *Metro Magazine*, 52: 14–17.

——— (2003), 'New Histories of the Kelly Gang: Gregor Jordan's Ned Kelly', *Senses of Cinema*, http://www.sensesofcinema.com/contents/03/26/ned_kelly.html. 14 July 2008.

——— (2007), 'The Impossible Dream: Hunt Angels', *Metro Magazine*, 151: 11–13.

Bertrand, Ina and William D. Routt (2007), *The Picture that Will Live Forever: The Story of the Kelly Gang*, Melbourne: Australian Teachers of Media (ATOM).

Block, Adam (2007), 'The Confessions of a Gay Rocker', in *The Rock History Reader*, edited by T. Cateforis. New York: Routledge: 185–193.

Blok, Anton (1974), *The Mafia of a Sicilian Village, 1860–1960: A Study of Violent Peasant Entrepeneurs*, Oxford: Blackwell.

Blystone, John G. (1925), *Dick Turpin*, America: Fox Film Corporation.

Boldrewood, Rolf (1882), *Robbery Under Arms*, Melbourne: Macmillan of Australia.

Bonanno, Massimo (1990), *The Rolling Stones Chronicle: The First Thirty Years*, North Ryde: Angus & Robertson.

Brampton, Kenneth (1920), *Robbery Under Arms*, Australia: Pacific Photo Plays.

Brown, Max (1948; 1956), *Australian Son*, Melbourne: Georgian House.

Bruce, Susan (1986), *A Treasury of Australian Bush Painting*, Hong Kong: Lloyd O' Neil.

Burn, David (1829), *The Bushrangers*, Melbourne: Heinemann.

——— (1974), *The Bushrangers*, Melbourne: Heinemann.

Burstall, Tim (1960), *Ned Kelly*, Australia: Melbourne Film-Makers Co-Op Ltd.

——— 1962. 'Man in Iron: Shooting Script', Melbourne: Eltham Film Productions.

Buzo, Alex (1988), 'Ned Kelly', in *The Young Person's Guide to the Theatre*, Melbourne: Penguin: 96–101.
Cammell, Donald and Nicolas Roeg (1970), *Performance*, England: Goodtimes Enterprises.
Campbell, Joseph (1973), *The Hero with a Thousand Faces*, New Jersey: Princeton University Press.
Carey, Peter (2000), *True History of the Kelly Gang*, St. Lucia: University of Queensland Press.
Cargill, Edna Griffiths (2000), *Glenrowan*, Croydon: Alice House Publishing and Art Gallery.
Carlyon, Les (1980), *The Last Outlaw*, Melbourne: HSV 7.
Carpenter, John (1979), *Elvis*, America: Dick Clark Productions.
Castieau, John Buckley (2004), In *The Difficulties of My Position: The Diaries of Prison Governor John Buckley Castieau, 1855–1884*, edited by M. Finnane, Canberra: National Library of Australia.
Castles, Alex C. (2005), *Ned Kelly's Last Days*, Crows Nest: Allen & Unwin.
Clark, Manning (1968), 'Good Day to You, Ned Kelly', in *Ned Kelly: Man and Myth*, edited by C. Cave, Melbourne: Cassell Australia: 12–39.
Clow, Robbit Jon (1919), *The Cause of the Kellys*, Ballarat: Baxter & Stubbs.
Cole, E. J. (1911), *The Five of Hearts, or Buffalo Bill's Love Story*, Australia: Edwin J. Cole's Bohemian Dramatic Company.
Corfield, Justin J. (2003), *The Ned Kelly Encyclopaedia*, Melbourne: Lothian Books.
Coulter, Michael (2006). 'The Ten Most Feared Sportsmen'. *The Sunday Age Sport* (26 March): 15.
Cranston, Jack (2006), *The Story of the Kelly Gang Film*, Glenrowan: Cobb & Co.
Crompton, Helen (1993). 'Seriously Patriotic'. *The Western Australian* (12 April): 5, 35.
Curtiz, Michael and William Keighley (1938), *The Adventures of Robin Hood*, America: Warner Bros. Pictures.
Danks, Adrian (2001), 'What's Been Puzzling You is the Nature of My Game', *Senses of Cinema*, 14, http://archive.sensesofcinema.com/contents/directors/07/tony-richardson.html.
Dawson, Jan (1970), 'Ned Kelly', *British Film Institute*, August: 159.
Delros, Marion (3 July 2005). 'Two of the Ned Kelly Gang Survived Ambush and Lived on for Years'. *Independent on Sunday* 25.
Dobson, Kevin James (1977), *Against the Wind*, Australia: Pegasus Productions.
Dominik, Andrew (2007), *The Assassination of Jesse James by the Coward Robert Ford*, America: Jesse Film Inc.
Donner, Clive (1969). *Alfred the Great*. England: Metro-Goldwyn-Mayer British Studios.
Drewe, Robert (1991), *Our Sunshine*, London: Penguin Books.
Dunstan, David (1996), *Victorian Icon: The Royal Exhibition Building*, Melbourne: Australian Scholarly Publishing.
Dylan, Bob (1968), *John Wesley Harding*, America: CBS.
Eggleston, Colin (1964–1975), *Homicide*, Australia: Crawford Productions.
Eimer, David (2003), 'Going Great Guns'. *The Sunday Times* (14 September): 15.
Engwerda, Robert, Richard Cotter and Maureen Anderson (eds) (2000), *Gold Diggers and Bushrangers, SOSE Studies of Society and Environment Australian History*, Queensland: John Wiley & Sons Australia.
Fahey, Warren (1975), *Joe Watson Australian Traditional Folk Singer*, Sydney: Australian Folklore Unit.

Farwell, George (1970), *Ned Kelly: The Life & Adventures of Australia's Notorious Bushranger*, Melbourne: Cheshire.
Ferrier, Susanne (1984), *Ned, A Leg End: A Thoroughly Misleading Account of His Life and Times*, Sydney: Collins.
Ford, John (1962), *The Man Who Shot Liberty Valance*, America: Paramount Pictures.
Forster, Marc (2001), *Monster's Ball*, America: Lions Gate Films.
Forsythe, Abe (2000), *Computer Boy*, Australia.
——— (2009), *Being Carl Williams*, Australia.
——— (2010), *Shock*, Australia.
Fotheringham, Richard (1987), 'The Man in the Iron Mask', *Cinema Papers*, 62: 32–36.
Frizell, Helen (1969). 'Jagger Stands Up to a Grilling'. *Sydney Morning Herald* (10 July): 6.
Frost, Warick (2006), 'Braveheart-ed Ned Kelly: Historic Films, Heritage Tourism and Destination Image', *Tourism Management*, 27: 247–254.
Gauci, John (1977a), *The Trial of Ned Kelly*, Australia: ABC.
——— (1977b), *The Trial of Ned Kelly*, Australia: ABC.
Gavan, Duffy, King, and King. *The Tait Brothers Intent to Screen the Movie*. nedonline.imageering.net.au 1906 [cited 4 September 2006].
Gavin, John (1928), *Trooper O'Brien*, Australia: Southern Cross Motion Pictures.
Gavin, John F. (1910), *Thunderbolt*, Australia: Southern Cross Motion Pictures.
——— (1911), *Ben Hall and His Gang*, Australia: Crick and Finlay.
Goad, Philip (1998), *Melbourne Architecture*, Balmain: The Watermark Press.
Gordon, Michael (1951), *Wherever She Goes*, Australia: Faun Films.
Hall, George Wilson (1878), *The Kelly Gang Or, The Outlaws of the Wombat Ranges*, Sydney: Australian History Promotions.
Hall, Ken G. (1946), *Smithy*, Australia: Columbia Pictures.
Hartrick, Elizabeth (2003), 'Consuming Illustrations: The Magic Lantern in Australia and Aotearoa/New Zealand 1850–1910' (Ph.D.), The Australian Centre, The University of Melbourne, Melbourne.
Haynes, Todd (2007), *I'm Not There*, America: Killer Films.
Hayter, Cecil (192?), 'Ned Kelly: A Tale of Trooper & Bushranger', in *The Boys' Friend Complete Library ; no. 44*, London: Amalgamated Press.
Helgeland, Brian (2001), *A Knight's Tale*, America: Columbia Pictures Corporation.
Hill, George Roy (1969). *Butch Cassidy and the Sundance Kid*. America: Campanile Productions.
Hobsbawm, Eric (1959), *Primitive Rebels: Studies in Archaic Forms of Social Movement in the 19th and 20th Centuries*, Manchester: Manchester University Press.
——— (2000), *Bandits*, London: Weidenfeld & Nicolson.
——— (2003), 'Inventing Traditions', in *The Invention of Tradition*, edited by E. Hobsbawm and T. Ranger. Cambridge: The Press Syndicate of The University of Cambridge.
Holden, Sergeant Keith (1968), 'Kelly – The Criminal', in *Ned Kelly: Man and Myth*, edited by C. Cave. Melbourne: Cassell: 190–199.
Holmes, Cecil (1955), *Captain Thunderbolt*, Australia: Associated Television.
Hughes, Robert (2003), *The Fatal Shore*, London: Vintage.
Hussein, Waris (1969), *Touch of Love*, England: Palomar Pictures International.

Ingram, Penelope (2006), 'Representing the Irish Body: Reading Red's Armour', *Antipodes*, 20. 1: 12–19.
Irvin, Eric (1981), 'Ridiculing the Police', in *Australian Melodrama*, Sydney: Hale & Iremonger: 78–85.
Jackson, Sally and Graham Shirley (2007), *The Story of the Kelly Gang – DVD Study Version*, Canberra: National Film & Sound Archive.
James, Elizabeth and Helen R. Smith (1998), *Penny Dreadfuls and Boys' Adventures: The Barry One Collection of Victorian Popular Literature in the British Library*, London: The British Library.
Jarmusch, Jim (1989), *Mystery Train*, America: JVC Entertainment Networks.
Jeffrey, Tom (1979), *The Odd Angry Shot*, Australia: Samson Productions.
Johnson, Dick (1977), *Bold Ned Kelly*, Melbourne: The Jabiru Press.
Johnson, Donald Hambleton (1995), *Horsemen Bold*, Glenrowan: Glen Rowen Cobb & Co. Pty. Ltd.
Jones, Ian (1968), 'A New View of Ned Kelly', in *Ned Kelly: Man and Myth*, edited by C. Cave, Melbourne: Cassell: 154–189.
——— (1977), 'Introduction', in *The Trial of Ned Kelly*, Melbourne: Heinemann Educational Australai Pty Ltd.
——— (1980), 'The Last Outlaw', *Cinema Papers*, 29, October-November: 352–354.
——— (1992), *The Fatal Friendship*, Melbourne: Lothian Books.
———, (2000), 'The Jerilderie Letter', *The La Trobe Journal*, Spring 66, 33–38.
———, (2002), *Ned Kelly: A Short Life*, Melbourne: Lothian Books.
———, (2005), 'Ned Kelly: 125 Years', Paper read at Faces of Kelly: A Forum (13 November), Australia: State Library of Victoria.
——— (2006), 'Jerilderie Letter', Paper read at Ned Kelly Event. Australia: State Library of Victoria.
Jones, Ian and Thomas Carrington (2003), *Ned Kelly: The Last Stand*, Melbourne: Lothian Books.
Jones, Ian and Glen Tomasetti (1968), 'Kelly – The Folk-Hero', in *Ned Kelly: Man and Myth*, edited by C. Cave. Melbourne: Cassell: 74–104.
Jones, Ross L. (2007), *Humanity's Mirror: 150 Years of Anatomy in Melbourne*, Melbourne University of Melbourne.
Jordan, Gregor (2001), *Buffalo Soldiers*, America: Gorilla Entertainment.
Kathner, Rupert (1945), *Let's Make a Movie: A Story of Picture Production in Australia*, Sydney: Currawong Publishing Company.
Kelly, Ned (1870), 'Letter to Sergeant James Babington', *Public Records Office Victoria*, VPRS 937/P Unit 272.
——— (1878), 'Letter to Mr Donald Cameron MLA', *Public Records Office Victoria*, VPRS 4966/P Unit 1.
——— (1879), 'Document known as the Jerilderie Letter', Australian Manuscripts Collection. State Library of Victoria: MS 13361.
Kelly, Veronica (ed.) (1997), *Annotated Calendar of Plays Premiered in Australia 1870–1890*, Queensland: University of Queensland.
Keneally, Thomas (1978), *Ned Kelly and the City of Bees*, London: Jonathan Cape.

Kenneally, J. J. (1969), *The Complete Inner History of the Kelly Gang and Their Pursuers*, 8th edition, Moe: The Kelly Gang Publishing Company Pty Ltd.

Kirsop, Wallace (1991), 'Barry's "Great Emporium" in the Twenty-First Century: The Future of The State Library of Victoria Collections', *The La Trobe Journal*, Spring, 46: 49–59.

Kitson, Jill (1981), 'The Last Outlaw', *Cinema Papers*, 31, March-April: 56–57.

Lee, Bevan (2001), *Always Greener*, Australia: Southern Star.

Livermore, Reg and Patrick Flynn (1978), *Ned Kelly: The Electric Music Show*, Australia: EMI.

Love, Harold (ed.) (1984), *The Australian Stage: A Documentary History*, Sydney: New South Wales University Press.

Lumet, Sidney (1973), *Serpico*, America: Produzioni De Laurentiis International.

Lundy, H. C. (1958), *Jerilderie 100 Years*, Jerilderie: Jerilderie Shire Council.

Lynn, Elwyn and Sidney Nolan (1985), *Sidney Nolan's Ned Kelly*, Canberra: Australian National Gallery.

Manifold, John (1964), *The Penguin Australian Song Book*, Ringwood: Penguin.

Mann, Delbert (1969). *David Copperfield*, England: 20th Century Fox Television.

Mansfield, Peter (2006), *Graham Berry: Geelong's Radical Premier*, Rippleside: Geelong Historical Society.

Marcus, Greil (1991), *Dead Elvis: A Chronicle of a Cultural Obsession*, New York: Doubleday.

——— (1997), *Mystery Train: Images of America in Rock 'N' Roll Music*, New York: A Plume Book.

Martin, Adrian (1994). 'Recklessly Seeking Serious Entertainment'. *The Mercury* (4 January): 52.

Matthews, Jill Julius (2005), *Dance Hall & Picture Palace: Sydney's Romance with Modernity*, Sydney: Currency Press.

McDonagh, John Michael (2003), *Ned Kelly The Screenplay*, Sydney: Currency Press.

McDonald, Neil (2003), 'Browyn Jones', *Quadrant*, 47, 6: 65–67.

McFarlane, Brian (1997), *An Autobiography of British Cinema*, Auckland: Random House.

——— (2006), 'Ned Kelly Rides Again … and Again', *Australian Screen Education*, 41, Summer: 24–32.

McIntyre, T. N. (1902), *A True Narrative of the Kelly Gang*, Melbourne: ms PA BOX 66, State Library of Victoria.

McKenna, Mark (1996), *The Captive Republic: A History of Republicanism in Australia 1788–1996*, Cambridge: Cambridge University Press.

McMenomy, Keith (2001), *Ned Kelly: The Authentic Illustrated History*, Melbourne: Hardie Grant Publishing.

McQuilton, John (1977), 'The Kelly Outbreak 1878–1880: The Geographical Dimension of Social Banditry' (Ph.D.), University of Melbourne, Melbourne.

——— (1979), *The Kelly Outbreak 1878–1880: The Geographical Dimension of Social Banditry*, Melbourne: Melbourne University Press.

——— (1982), 'Australian Bushranging and Social Banditry with Special Reference to the Kelly Outbreak', *Royal Geographical Society of Australasia*, 83, 48–63.

——— (1988), 'Police in Rural Victoria: A Regional Example', in *Policing in Australia: Historical Perspectives*, edited by M. Finnane. Kensington: University of New South Wales: 35–58.

Megaw, Ruth (1968) 'The American Image: Influence on Australia Cinema Management', *Journal of the Royal Australian Historical Society* (54.2): 194–204.
Middleton, Hannah (1977), *But Now We Want the Land Back*, Sydney: New Age Publishers.
Midnight Oil (1981), 'If Ned Kelly Was King', in *Place Without A Postcard*, Australia: Sony.
Molitorisz, Sacha (2003). 'This is a Send-Up'. *Sydney Morning Herald (Metro)* (23 May): 4.
Molony, John (2001), *Ned Kelly*, Melbourne: Melbourne University Press.
Mora, Philippe (1976), *Mad Dog Morgan*, Australia: Motion Picture Productions.
Morgan, Alec (2006), *Hunt Angels*, Australia: Hunt Angels Productions Pty Ltd.
Mudie, Peter (1997), *Ubu Films: Sydney Underground Movies 1965–1970*, Sydney: UNSW Press.
Murphy, Jim (1980). 'The Last Outlaw – A Loving Look At', *The Australian Women's Weekly* 4.
Noonan, Michael (1960), *Whiplash*, Australia: 7 Network.
O'Brien, John (1925), *The Outlaw's Daughter*, America: Universal Pictures.
O'Farrell, Patrick (2000), *The Irish in Australia: 1788 to the Present*, Sydney: University of New South Wales Press.
O'Shea, Helen (2005), 'New-Age Ned: Scoring Irishness and Masculinity in Ned Kelly', in *Reel Tracks: Australian Feature Film Music and Cultural Identities*, edited by R. Coyle, Malaysia: John Libbey Publishing: 35–47.
Oldis, Ken (2000), 'The True Story of the Kelly Armour', *The La Trobe Journal*, 66, Spring: 38–48.
——— (2008), *The Chinawoman*, Melbourne: Australian Scholarly Publishing Pty Ltd.
Peacock, A. J., *Prohibition of Performance*. nedonline.imagineering.net.au 2006 [cited September 4, 2006].
Peckinpah, Sam (1973), *Pat Garrett & Billy the Kid*, America: Metro-Goldwyn-Mayer (MGM).
Penn, Arthur (1967), *Bonnie and Clyde*, America: Tatira-Hiller Productions.
Perry, David E. (1968), *Mad Mesh*, Australia: Ubu Films.
Perry, Joseph (1904), *Bushranging in North Queensland*, Australia: Limelight Department.
Pike, Andrew and Ross Cooper (1980), *Australian Film 1900–1977*, Melbourne: Oxford University Press.
Plato (2007), In *The Torso in the Canal: The Inside Story on Ireland's Most Grotesque Killing*, edited by J. Mooney. Dunshaughlin: Maverick House.
Porter, Edwin (1903), *The Great Train Robbery*, America: Edison Manufacturing Company.
Pratt, Ambrose (ed.) (1911), *Dan Kelly Outlaw: Memoirs*, Sydney: Alfred Cecil Rowlandson.
Presland, Gary (1994), 'Chinese Detectives', *Journal of Police History*, 2.1: 49–53.
——— (1998), *For God's Sake Send the Trackers: A History of Queensland Trackers and Victoria Police*, Melbourne: Victoria Press.
Pullen, Roland (1971). 'A Place in the Paris Sun'. *The Sun* 9.
Pybus, Cassandra (2002), 'Black Caesar', *Arena Magazine*, 57. February–March: 30–34.
Rawlins, Adrian (1969), 'Ned Kelly in Two Dimensions', *Go-Set*, 9.
Ray, Nicholas (1953), *Rebel Without a Cause*, America: Warner Bros Pictures.
Read, Aggy (1968), *Boobs a Lot*, Australia: Ubu Films.
Reade, Eric (1970), *Australian Silent Films*, Melbourne: Lansdowne Press.
——— (1972), *The Talkies Era*, Melbourne: Lansdowne Press.
——— (1975), *The Australian Screen; A Pictorial History of Australian Film Making*, Melbourne Lansdowne.

——— (1979), *History and Heartburn: The Saga of Australian Film 1896–1978*, Sydney: Harper & Row Publishers.
Reisz, Karel (1964), *Night Must Fall*, England: Metro-Goldwyn-Mayer British Studios.
Richardson, Tony (1963), *Tom Jones*, England: Woodfall Film Productions.
——— (1968), *The Charge of the Light Brigade*, England: Woodfall Film Productions.
——— (1969a), *Hamlet*, England: Woodfall Film Productions.
——— (1969b), *Laughter in the Dark*, Woodfall Film Productions, Winkast Film Productions.
Riddett, Tobyn and Geoffrey Down (1991), *The Old Melbourne Gaol*, Melbourne: The National Trust.
Rolling Stones, The (1968), *Beggars Banquet*, England: Decca.
Rose, Deborah Bird (1994), 'Ned Kelly Died for Our Sins', *Oceania*, 65:2: 175–187.
Rosenfeld, Dorothy (1934). 'And the Kellys Ride Again'. *The Photoplayer* (10 February): 17–18.
Rosenstone, Robert (1988), 'History in Images/History in Words', *The American Historical Review*, 98:5.
Ross, Stewart (1995), *Fact or Fiction: Bandits & Outlaws*, London: Aladdin Books Ltd.
Routt, William D. (1999a), 'The Kelly Gang', in *The Oxford Companion to Australian Film*, edited by B. McFarlane, G. Mayer and I. Bertrand. Melbourne: Oxford University Press.
——— (1999b), 'The Story of the Kelly Gang', in *The Oxford Companion to Australian Film*, edited by B. McFarlane, G. Mayer and I. Bertrand, Melbourne: Oxford University Press.
——— (2001) *More Australian than Aristotelian: The Australian Bushranger Film, 1904–1914*. http://www.sensesofcinema.com/contents/01/18/oz_western.html, December 2001 [cited 23 September 2005].
——— (2003a), 'Bush Westerns?: The Lost Genre', Paper read at State Library of Victoria.
——— (2003b), 'The Kelly Films', Paper read at Still Riding On: The Kelly Influence Conference 7 May. State Library of Victoria.
——— (2003c), 'Red Ned', *Metro Magazine*, 136:6: 10–17.
Roxon, Lillian (1970). 'Pop Star Fizzes as Ned Kelly'. *Sun-Herald* (21 June): 21.
Rutherford, Graeme (1971), 'Iron Outlaw and Steel Sheila'. *Sunday Observer* (28 February): 9.
Sadleir, John (1913), *Recollections of a Victorian Police Officer*, Melbourne: G Robertson.
Sanderson, Martyn, Mick Glasheen and John Allen (1970), *A Stone in the Bush*, Australia: Filmmakers Co-operatives.
Saura, Carlos (1964), *Llanto por un bandido/Weeping for a Bandit*, Spain: Atlantica Cinematografica Produzione Films.
Schepisi, Fred (1978), *Chant of Jimmy Blacksmith*, Australia: The Film House.
Seal, Graham (1980), *Game as Ned Kelly: The Folklore of an Australian Legend*, Paddington: Larrikin Records.
——— (1989), *The Hidden Culture: Folklore in Australian Society*, Melbourne: Oxford University Press.
——— (1990), *Traditions of Prejudice*, Perth: The Antipodes Press.
——— (1993), 'The Wild Colonial Boy Rides Again and Again', *Australian Studies*, 7: 161–172.
——— (1996), *The Outlaw Legend*, Cambridge: Cambridge University Press.
——— (2002), *Tell 'em I Died Game*, Melbourne: Hyland House.
——— (2005), *Echoes of Anzac: The Voice of Australians at War*, South Melbourne: Lothian Books.

Serious, Yahoo (1988), *Young Einstein*, Serious Productions: Australia.
——— (1993), *Reckless Kelly*, Australia: Larrikin Films/Serious Entertainment/Warner Brothers.
——— (2000), *Mr Accident*, Australia: Serious Entertainment.
Shead, Gary (1967), *Stringybark Massacre*, Australia: Sydney Filmmakers Co-operative.
Shirley, Graham and Brian Adams (1983), *Australian Cinema: The First Eighty Years*, Sydney: Angus & Robertson.
Sterling, William (1960), *Ned Kelly*, Australia: Australian Broadcast Corporation.
Stewart, Douglas (1943), *Ned Kelly*, Sydney: Angus and Robertson.
Stewart, Douglas and Nancy Keesing (eds) (1955), *Australian Bush Ballads*, Sydney: Angus and Robertson.
Stewart, Paul (1997). 'Black and White of Mick'. *Sunday Herald Sun* (9 November): 92.
Stratton, David (2003). 'Ned'. *Variety* (23 May).
Sutherland, Claire (2002), 'Heath of the Moment'. *Herald Sun* (4 May): 12.
Tait, John and Nevin Tait (1906), *The Story of the Kelly Gang: Theatre Programme*, Melbourne: Syd. Day.
Tait, Viola (1971), 'The Kelly Gang', in *A Family of Brothers*, Melbourne: Heinemann.
Taylor, Charles E. (1929), *The Girl Who Helped Ned Kelly*, Melbourne: United Press.
Thoms, Albie (1978), *Polemics for a New Cinema*, Glebe, N.S.W: Wild & Woolley.
Thornhill, Michael (1970). 'Ned Kelly'. *The Australian* (25 August).
Tilse, Tony (2008), *Underbelly*, Australia: Nine Network Australia.
Tulloch, John (1981), *Legends of the Screen*, Sydney: Currency Press.
Urban, Andrew L. (1993), 'Yahoo Serious Reckless Kelly', *Cinema Papers*, 92, April: 31–35, 72.
Verhoeff, Nanna (2006), *The West in Early Cinema: After the Beginning*, Amsterdam: Amsterdam University Press.
Wachowski, Andy and Lana Wachowski (1999), *The Matrix*, America: Warner Bros. Pictures.
Watson, Joe (1976), *Ballad of the Kelly Gang*, Australia: (Sound Recording) Larrikin Records.
Weir, Peter (1975), *Picnic at Hanging Rock*, Australia: McElroy & McElroy.
Whitaker, Robert (1970), *Mick Jagger is Ned Kelly*, London: Hunt Barnard.
White, Hayden (1978), *Tropics of Discourse: Essays in Cultural Criticism*, Baltimore: John Hopkins University Press.
Whitlams, The (2002), *Kate Kelly*, Australia: (Sound Recording) Black Yak Records.
Williams, Deane (2008), *An Arc of Mirrors: Australian Post-War Documentary Film*, Bristol: Intellect Books.
Willis, Anne-Marie (1988), *Picturing Australia: A History of Photography*, London: Angus and Robertson.
Woods, Carole (1985), *Beechworth: A Titan's Field*, North Melbourne: Hargreen Publishing Company.
Wyman, Bill (2002), *Rolling with the Stones*, London: Dorling Kindersley Limited.
Zachariah, Richard (2001), 'He's a Perfect Fit'. *Sunday Telegraph* (2 December): 28.
Zwar, Adam (2000), 'Mick's Flop in Kelly Country'. *Sunday Herald Sun* (2 April): 83.
——— (2002), 'Mick and the Kelly Curse'. *Sunday Herald Sun* (13 January): 36.

Index